BERKELEY

Real-estate poster shows Berkeley in 1891, seen west from the hills. Open spaces still separate the old Ocean View from the rest of the town. Shattuck Avenue, with its steam train line, is establishing itself as Berkeley's downtown.

BERKELEY
A CITY IN HISTORY

CHARLES WOLLENBERG

UNIVERSITY OF CALIFORNIA PRESS
BERKELEY LOS ANGELES LONDON

The publisher gratefully acknowledges the generous contribution to this book provided by the Humanities Endowment Fund of the University of California Press Foundation.

University of California Press, one of the most distinguished university presses in the United States, enriches lives around the world by advancing scholarship in the humanities, social sciences, and natural sciences. Its activities are supported by the UC Press Foundation and by philanthropic contributions from individuals and institutions. For more information, visit www.ucpress.edu.

University of California Press
Berkeley and Los Angeles, California

University of California Press, Ltd.
London, England

Library of Congress Cataloging-in-Publication Data

Wollenberg, Charles.
    Berkeley : a city in history / Charles M. Wollenberg.
       p.   cm.
    Includes bibliographical references and index.
    ISBN 978-0-520-25307-0 (cloth : alk. paper)
    1. Berkeley (Calif.)—History.   2. Berkeley (Calif.)—
Social conditions.   I. Title.
  F869.B5W65   2007
979.4'67—dc22   2007022332

Manufactured in Canada

17 16 15 14 13 12 11 10 09 08
10 9 8 7 6 5 4 3 2 1

This book is printed on New Leaf EcoBook 50, a 100% recycled fiber of which 50% is de-inked post-consumer waste, processed chlorine-free. EcoBook 50 is acid-free and meets the minimum requirements of ANSI/ASTM D5634–01 (*Permanence of Paper*).

CONTENTS

ILLUSTRATIONS

PREFACE

This book is based on a class I have occasionally taught at the Berkeley Public Library through Vista College (now Berkeley City College). An early version of the manuscript, without illustrations, is on the library's website and has served as the class text. Neither the class nor the book was intended to be a comprehensive chronicle of Berkeley's past. Instead I have tried to present an impressionistic survey of the city's history, giving residents a sense of how their hometown developed and how their individual experiences and those of their families, neighborhoods, and communities fit into a larger historical framework. For nonresidents, the book discusses the history of a city that, given its modest size, has had a remarkable influence on the state, the nation, and even the world. Few American cities of a hundred thousand people are as famous (or infamous) as Berkeley, California.

Unlike some local histories, this book is not an exercise in nostalgia. Nostalgia is a perfectly good human emotion, but it doesn't make for very good history. The nostalgic view of the past accentuates the positive and all but eliminates the negative. It assumes a separation between past and present that allows one to avoid the cares and woes of today by escaping into the good old days of yesteryear. But the good old days weren't always so good—or, in Berkeley's case, so old. Berkeley's existence as an English-speaking American community goes back only 150 years, barely two lifetimes. Most of our community's contemporary problems have their roots in the not-so-distant past, and many important historical themes are alive and well today, still very much affecting contemporary Berkeley society.

The nostalgic approach also separates a community's history from its broad context by emphasizing only the unique and special, in effect arguing that the city is a creation of its own self-generated past. This is an appealing argument in Berkeley's case, because much of the city's culture and experience are indeed unusual, even unique. But Berkeley, like any other American community, has been significantly shaped by forces beyond its city limits. This book, then, is dedicated to the proposition that Berkeley is "a city in history," that its past and present can be understood only in the context of national, state, and regional historical themes. To paraphrase a slogan of the environmental movement, Berkeley historians need to think globally but write locally.

Given the role of the Berkeley Public Library in the development of the course and this book, it is not surprising that I owe a special debt of gratitude to several members of the library staff. This is particularly true of Jane Scantlebury, whose support and assistance over the years has been invaluable. Other library folks who contributed greatly to the endeavor are Sayre Van Young, Bob Saunderson, Geraldine Ewart, and Andrea Segall. I am also indebted to Dick Walker and Steve Finacom of the University of California, Berkeley, for their close critical reading of the manuscript and their many helpful suggestions. Jerry Herman, Linda Rosen, and Malcolm Margolin also read all or parts of the text and gave me valuable feedback. At the University of California Press, I especially benefited from the support and assistance of editors Randy Heyman and Kate Warne. Finally, I must acknowledge the good work of the staff of the Bancroft Library and the efforts of the many active volunteers of the Berkeley Historical Society and the Berkeley Architectural Heritage Association, who labor long and hard to keep the city's past alive.

CHAPTER ONE

FIRST SETTLERS

In the year 2000 the Berkeley city council approved formal land-mark status for the Indian shellmound that once stood near the mouth of Strawberry Creek in West Berkeley. Scientists estimate that the mound, actually a giant midden filled with the debris and material remnants of the society that created it, was used for more than three thousand years, from 3000 B.C. to A.D. 800. Like dozens of similar features along the San Francisco Bay shore, the Berke-ley shellmound was leveled and paved over in the late nineteenth and early twentieth centuries. But some traces of the structure sur-vive under the Truitt and White lumberyard and the Spenger's Restaurant parking lot. Vociferous opponents of the landmark pro-posal, mainly property owners concerned about what they saw as overly restrictive limits on development, argued that the site was not eligible for landmark status because it was "archaeological" rather than "historical," although the precise difference between these categories is not entirely clear. At any rate, the city council's approval, after some heated debate and discussion, implicitly rec-ognizes the fact that Berkeley's history begins not with the arrival of American residents a hundred and fifty years ago but extends back thousands of years to the area's very first settlers.

THE HUICHIN

When the Europeans arrived in the late eighteenth century, Berkeley was inhabited by the Huichin, part of the larger Ohlone or Costanoan linguistic and cultural group which occupied coastal regions from the central Bay Area south to Monterey Bay. Like all Ohlone peoples, the Huichin lived in bands of a few hundred individuals inhabiting a well-defined hunting and gathering territory. Their villages were collections of small, conical-shaped thatch houses, often surrounding larger public and ceremonial structures. Although they made no use of metals, the Huichin manufactured a great variety of tools, implements, and household goods, including sophisticated baskets woven so tightly they could be used to store water.

The Huichin hunted rabbits and other small rodents, a well as deer, elk, and antelope. They snared migratory birds in the vast marshlands that once bordered San Francisco Bay and gathered shellfish from the mud flats and tidelands. They caught trout, steelhead, and salmon in freshwater streams and navigated the bay in thatch boats propelled by double-bladed paddles. Although they were hardly pacifists, their warfare took the limited form of feuds and retaliatory raids on neighboring peoples rather than all-out campaigns of conquest and domination.

The Huichin lived lightly on the land, but by no means invisibly. They burned grasslands to promote the growth of edible plants and dug up meadows to harvest roots and tubers. They trimmed trees and bushes to stimulate the growth of twigs and leaves for basket making and gathered huge harvests of acorns, which, when ground into meal, formed their diet staple. The work of countless generations of Huichin women, grinding acorns and other seeds and nuts, produced deep indentations in rock formations that are still visible in Mortar Rock Park in North Berkeley. As the author Malcolm Margolin put it in his book *The Ohlone Way*, before the arrival of Europeans "the Bay Area was a deeply inhabited environment, and its landscape bore the cultural imprint of its people as surely as did the farmlands of Europe or New England."

The shellmounds, created by peoples who may have preceded the Huichin by centuries, were among the most dramatic of these "imprints." When twentieth-century University of California anthropologists examined the layers of material deposited in the mounds, they found a record of the evolution of Indian material culture over thousands of years. Although the scientists found evidence of significant transformations in tool making, diet, and other cultural forms over the centuries, from our twenty-first century perspective it is remarkable how little life seems to have changed. When the Spaniards arrived in the 1770s, the Huichin were living in much the same way that people had lived on these shores three thousand years earlier, at the time of the Trojan War.

The Huichin had achieved a successful adaptation to the environment and saw little reason for rapid change. They apparently understood the principle of agriculture, but, given the abundance of wild food sources, found no need to practice it (except, possibly, for the cultivation of a strain of wild tobacco whose use would be frowned on by health-conscious contemporary Berkeleyans). The Huichin way of life emphasized continuity and tradition. They were certainly familiar with their neighbors and participated in complex trading networks that stretched for hundreds of miles, but the Huichin were, in the author Theodora Kroeber's words, "true provincials." They knew the landscape of their particular hunting and gathering territory with an intimacy and specificity that modern Californians can scarcely comprehend. To say the Huichin were "settlers" of the land that was to become Berkeley is an understatement. They were linked to that land by the most central elements of life, spirit, and culture.

SPANISH COLONIALISM

The beginning of the end of the Huichin way of life came when Captain Gaspar de Portolá made the first European contact with San Francisco Bay in 1769. Ordered by the Spanish colonial authorities in Mexico City to establish settlements in California, Portolá and a small band of soldiers were looking for Monterey Bay, but they walked right by it and stumbled on San Francisco Bay instead. They retreated and finally recognized Monterey, establishing settlements there in 1770. Two years later, California governor Pedro Fages led an exploratory expedition along San Francisco Bay's eastern shore and may have camped on the banks of Strawberry Creek, possibly near what today is the West Gate of the University of California campus, where a monument commemorates the event.

In 1776, Captain Juan Bautista de Anza founded the first Spanish-speaking settlement on the bay. The Spanish advance into California was an exercise in defensive expansion—an attempt to prevent rival European colonial powers from occupying the area. Anza thus picked an ideal defensive location—a mesa overlooking the Golden Gate, named the San Francisco Presidio, which remained a military post until the end of the twentieth century. The first religious and agricultural institution, Mission Dolores, was also located on the west side of the bay. Not until 1797 was a settlement established on the east side of the bay—Mission San Jose, in what is now southern Alameda County. By then, the East Bay was already called "contra costa," the opposite or other shore (now the name of an adjoining East Bay county). As early as the 1790s, the implication was that *the* shore, the site of the action and power, was the San Francisco side of the bay.

Unlike the New England colonies, where English-speaking people came in relatively large numbers to work the land and drive the native peoples out, Spain sent very few Spanish-speaking people to a new colony such as California. The Spanish came as the ruling class, the colonial masters, and the work was done by the colonial subjects, the native peoples. For the Spanish colony to succeed, the Indians had to be integrated into the new society as manual and agricultural workers. But in the Bay Area, as in most of California, the Indians were hunting and gathering peoples whose way of life had little in common with that of the Spanish Empire. Spain intended not only to conquer and Christianize the Huichin but also to change their entire culture and transform them into an agricultural people who could cultivate fields, tend stock, and practice European crafts.

To accomplish this daunting task, the Spanish brought to California what by 1769 was a tried and true colonial institution, the mission. The mission was certainly intended to Christianize the Indians and save their souls, but the Franciscan friars also disciplined and organized the Indians and taught them the skills, habits, and attitudes of an effective colonial working class. The missions intended to destroy most of the Indian way of life; they ended up unintentionally destroying most of the Indian people as well. On and around the missions, Indians contracted European diseases to which they had little or no immunity, and the death rate soared. The Huichin were stricken by disease as early as the 1780s, as Mission Dolores recruited Huichin converts and mission livestock was introduced onto Huichin territory. By 1820 there seem to have been no more native people left in what today is Berkeley. A terrible process of decimation through colonialization left areas that had been extensively populated for at least three thousand years essentially empty of human habitation.

Along with the mission, the Spanish also brought the presidio, or frontier fort, to California. Although only four formal presidios were established (at San Diego, Monterey, San Francisco, and Santa Barbara), soldiers were part of every Spanish-speaking settlement. Each mission and pueblo (civilian town) had a detachment of soldiers to protect against Indian uprising and enforce the authority of the Franciscan friars. Most of the Spanish-speaking settlers in colonial California were thus soldiers and their families. Included in this group were Corporal Gabriel Peralta and his family, who came to the Bay Area as part of the Anza expedition of 1776. Like most of the "Spanish" settlers in California, the Peraltas were in fact natives of northwestern Mexico. Of ethnically mixed background and something less than upper-class origins, people like the Peraltas were the founding fathers and mothers of Spanish California. No matter what their social status had been in Mexico, they were, by definition, the new colony's elite.

The Peralta family included Gabriel's seventeen-year-old son, Luis, who in the early 1780s followed in his father's footsteps and joined the army. He was destined to serve about forty years before finally mustering out as a sergeant. Although he was stationed at many different posts during his long military career, Peralta finished his service in the garrison of the pueblo of San Jose, where he became one of the leading citizens. In 1818 he asked the governor for an extensive land grant as a reward for his long service on the king's behalf. Because there was no appropriate land available near San Jose, in 1820 Peralta accepted what became Rancho San Antonio, a 48,000-acre grant extending from San Leandro Creek in the south to El Cerrito (Albany Hill) in the north. Peralta thus became master of an area that today includes Oakland, Alameda, Piedmont, Emeryville, Albany, and part of San Leandro, as well as all of Berkeley.

Don Luis elected to live in San Jose for the remainder of his very long life and sent his four sons north to occupy and operate Rancho San Antonio. The brothers informally divided the grant between themselves, Ignacio and Antonio occupying the southern portion and Vicente and Domingo settling in the north. For a while, Vicente, Domingo, and their large families lived together in an adobe home in what is now Oakland's Temescal district. But in 1841, Domingo, now in his forties and blessed (or burdened) with ten children, decided it was high time to establish a home of his own. On the bank of Codornices Creek, near the entrance of today's St. Mary's High School, Domingo built a modest adobe house with a tile roof and dirt floor which became the first European-style dwelling in what is today Berkeley. Ten years later, he moved into a larger wood-framed home nearby. The original adobe was destroyed in the 1868 earthquake, but the wooden structure survived until the 1930s, when it was torn down to make way for an apartment house.

In 1842 Don Luis formally divided the rancho among his four sons, with Domingo receiving title to the northernmost portion—roughly Albany, Berkeley, and most of Emeryville. The original 48,000-acre allotment was larger than most local land grants, but Domingo's ten or twelve thousand acres was about the average size for a California rancho. He probably grazed between 1,500 and 2,000 head of cattle on his property, the precise number varying with the market and the weather.

Operations of the rancho inevitably affected the natural environment. Competition for pasture by rancho cattle reduced the great herds of elk and antelope that once grazed in the East Bay flatlands. Intensive cattle grazing also destroyed the native perennial bunch grasses. They were replaced by nonnative annuals whose seeds were inadvertently imported from Mexico on the hooves of livestock. The Peraltas dug wells and diverted streams for irrigation and domestic purposes, and the absence of traditional Huichin burning and food-gathering practices promoted new patterns of native plant growth and distribution. By the 1840s, the very landscape had dramatically changed.

The Peralta property was a typical California rancho in all but one respect: the fact that the original land grant was made during Spanish rule. From 1769 to 1821, California was a colony of Spain, and the Spanish government made about twenty land grants to individuals, including Luis Peralta. From 1821 to 1846, California was part of the independent nation of Mexico, and the Mexican government made between six and eight hundred California land grants. (To assure the validity of his holding, Don Luis had Rancho San Antonio regranted under Mexican law in 1824.) Virtually all the fabled old Spanish ranchos were in reality new Mexican land grants. Indeed, the majority of Mexican grants were made after 1833, when the mission system was dismantled and the land and labor force it had controlled became available for private distribution.

In the 1830s, then, the Peraltas began to have neighbors. To the south, the Estudillo family established Rancho San Leandro; to the north, the Castros founded Rancho San Pablo. Over the hills to the east, the Moragas and Bernals shared Rancho de la Laguna de los Palos Colorados (Ranch of the Redwood-Tree Lagoon). In economic terms, the rancho had replaced the mission as the central institution of Hispanic California, and land-holding families like the Peraltas had replaced the missionary friars as the most powerful people in the province.

Although their lifestyle and lineage were exceedingly modest compared to those of the great landed families of Mexico or Spain, California rancheros like the Peraltas played the role of aristocrats, entertaining lavishly, acting as generous hosts, and expecting deference. Small in stature and dark in complexion like his father, Domingo was described as friendly and courteous but "with an impulsive nature" that could manifest itself in moody and argumentative behavior.

The ranchos represented the beginning of capitalism in California. During the Spanish period, the friars used the land and labor primarily to support and feed the mission population and maintain the colony's self-sufficiency. The ranchos, by contrast, were private property, occupied and worked to make a profit and accumulate wealth. Cattle hides and tallow (fat) were the major agricultural products, but Mexico already had plenty of both. So the Peraltas and their fellow rancheros developed foreign markets in places like the eastern United States and Britain, which needed hides to manufacture leather goods and tallow to make soap and candles. American and British ships sailed around Cape Horn to California, trading manufactured items and luxury goods for the hides and tallow. The exchange inevitably led to a small but influential English-speaking community in California—mainly young Americans who served as middlemen in the trade. The Peraltas dealt extensively with William Heath Davis, a Yankee whose published memoir is one of our best primary sources on the masters of Rancho San Antonio.

DECLINE AND FALL OF THE PERALTAS

By the time Domingo Peralta built his adobe on Codornices Creek in 1841, California was already trading more with New York and Boston than with Mexico City, Acapulco, or San Blas. In a sense, the American military conquest of California during the U.S.-

Mexican War (1846–48) was anticlimactic: California had already been integrated into the American economic sphere of influence. The war and subsequent change in political status seemed to have little impact on the Peraltas. For them and for most of their fellow Spanish-speaking Californios, real change came as a result of the discovery of gold in the Sierra foothills in early 1848. By 1849 the Gold Rush was under way, and, in the words of the author J. S. Holliday, "the world rushed in."

No place was more dramatically transformed by the Gold Rush than San Francisco. A village of five or six hundred people in early 1848, San Francisco was a city of twenty-five thousand by the end of 1849. It kept growing in the 1850s, emerging as the major urban core of Gold Rush California, and then as a center of economic and social influence. No city has so thoroughly dominated an American region as San Francisco dominated the Far West in the three decades following the Gold Rush. The Peralta land grant, located just a few miles across the bay, was inevitably affected by this remarkable urban growth.

When the Gold Rush began, Luis Peralta, then in his nineties, advised his sons to let the Americans go after the treasure. "You can go to your ranch and raise grain, and that will be your best gold, because we all must eat while we live." His words are sometimes cited as evidence of the old man's wisdom, but, as it turned out, Don Luis couldn't have given his sons worse advice. They did indeed try to stay with the land, but the land did not stay with them. The Peraltas depended on provisions of the 1848 Treaty of Guadalupe Hidalgo, which ended the war with Mexico and transferred control of California to the United States. It stipulated that the American government recognize and protect the property rights of former Mexican citizens such as the Peraltas. In addition, the Californios were made American citizens, with all the constitutional protections, including guarantees of property rights, that citizenship conveys. But these treaty obligations and constitutional protections ran head-on into the American tradition of squatter's rights, the idea that a person could obtain title to vacant land simply by occupying it. This practice was strengthened in 1851, when the California legislature passed a law allowing an American citizen to preempt up to 160 acres of land, providing that "to the best of his knowledge and belief" the land did not belong to someone else. In 1852 Francis Kittredge Shattuck, a disappointed gold seeker from upstate New York, and his partners, George Blake, William Hillegass, and James Leonard, each filed 160-acre claims on what is now central Berkeley. (It's hard to imagine that they did not have "knowledge and belief" of the existence of the thirty-two-year-old Peralta grant.) Further west, the Irish immigrant Michael Curtis was farming near Domingo Peralta's home. In that same year, 1852, Domingo was arrested for assaulting two squatters with a sword. He was found guilty and fined seven hundred dollars for the offense, but nothing was done to remove the squatters.

To attempt to clarify the confused state of property rights, Congress established the California Land Commission in 1851. In the following year, the three-man commission began meeting in San Francisco to try to determine who owned what land in California. Grant holders like the Peraltas were required to appear before the body and submit proof of their claims. The burden of proof was thus on the rancheros, and the families had to hire lawyers to present their cases. Nevertheless, the Peralta brothers were among the first to appear, and within two years the commission confirmed Domingo's title. A commission decision could be appealed to federal district court, and in almost all cases, including the Peraltas', the appeal was made. Overworked U.S. federal judges found themselves trying to determine whether grants made in the 1820s, 30s, and 40s conformed to the provisions of

FIGURE 1. Francis Kittredge Shattuck, an early squatter on Peralta land, became one of Berkeley's leading businessmen and the developer of the city's downtown. Bancroft Library, University of California, Berkeley.

complicated Spanish and Mexican laws. When the district court finally made its ruling (often after several years of deliberation), the matter could be further appealed. The Peralta cases were among the dozens that made it all the way to the U.S. Supreme Court.

While the claims were winding their painful way through the federal court system, other legal conflicts often intervened. After Luis Peralta's death, his five daughters sued their brothers, claiming that the Peralta land grant should have been allocated to all nine children, not just the four sons. Even after such family conflicts were resolved and the federal courts finally approved a land grant, disagreements over the precise boundaries could provoke further legal conflicts. During the Spanish and Mexican periods, the grants were defined by crude maps called *disenos*, which showed the broad limits of the territory in relation to easily recognized landmarks. Errors of a few yards one way or another seemed unimportant. But under U.S. law, precise surveys were required. The northern and eastern boundaries of the Peralta grant also formed the northern and eastern boundaries of Alameda County, which had separated from Contra Costa in 1852. Some of the earliest photographs of Berkeley were taken in connection with court-ordered surveys to resolve the legal conflicts over Peralta boundaries. The legal processes were so complex that the average land-grant case took seventeen years to resolve. The Peralta cases dragged on from 1852 until 1877.

For Domingo and his brothers, this process proved disastrous. Already contending with squatters and cattle rustlers, the Peraltas also had to pay a seemingly endless series of lawyers' bills and a new phenomenon in California life—property taxes. In such circumstances, it is hardly surprising that the brothers looked for the best deals they could find to escape from their landowners' woes. In 1853, Domingo sold a small part of his holding to John Fleming. (That plot, now a portion of the Golden Gate Fields racetrack property, came to be known as Fleming Point.) Later that same year, Domingo sold the rest of his land, with the exception of a three-hundred-acre tract surrounding his homestead, to a group of prominent San Francisco investors led by the attorney Hall McAllister. With their political influence and economic clout, the investors could force squatters like Shattuck to pay market value to regularize their titles. Although Domingo received $82,000 for his land, this sum barely paid his debts, and later in the 1850s, his three hundred acres were seized because he was unable to meet his financial obligations. He sold another hundred acres and retrieved the remainder of the parcel, but, at the time of his death in 1865, Domingo's family was unable to pay his burial fee at St. Mary's Cemetery in Oakland. In 1872, Domingo's heirs were evicted from their home, and the family lost what was left of their Berkeley property.

In 1877, the courts finally resolved all the issues in the Peralta land case. After twenty-five years of litigation, the Peraltas won on all counts. The original land grant was valid, only the four sons were Don Luis's rightful heirs, and the boundaries were essentially those originally claimed by the Peraltas. But although the family had won the legal battle, it had long since lost the land war. By 1877, the Peraltas controlled almost nothing of the original 48,000-acre grant. Technically, the land hadn't been stolen, but unfriendly legal processes and a hostile social and economic environment made it impossible for the family to hold Rancho San Antonio or significantly profit from its sale. Developers and speculators—men like Shattuck, whose title now depended on the validity of the original grant—were the real winners. By 1877 the university had already moved to its Berkeley campus, and the city was just one year away from formal incorporation. For residents of the new community, it was an era of great possibilities, but the first settlers, Huichins and Peraltas alike, were gone and soon forgotten.

CHAPTER TWO

A TALE OF TWO TOWNS

Berkeley had not one but two beginnings. Two separate communities, with very different roots and traditions, formally came together on April Fools' Day 1878 to establish the city of Berkeley. The social, economic, and cultural differences between those communities and the political conflicts they engendered have shaped Berkeley history ever since. When Berkeleyans distinguish between the hills and the flats, East Berkeley and West Berkeley, or town and gown, they are referring in part to divisions that derive from the city's dual origins.

OCEAN VIEW

The first of the founding communities was Ocean View, an informal, unincorporated settlement located along the bay shore, immediately north and south of the mouth of Strawberry Creek. The key to its existence was the decision of Captain James Jacobs to anchor his sloop at the creek's mouth in 1853.

By that time, the Bay Area was already becoming a metro-

FIGURE 2. Berkeley wharf, ca. 1890. The original pier built on this water-front by James Jacobs in the 1850s began the development of Ocean View. Berkeley Historical Society, Berkeley, CA.

politan region, with a number of small communities developing around the bay to provide goods and services to San Francisco. Access to the bay was crucial, as it was the region's chief transportation and communication route, linking outlying communities with San Francisco's urban core. A native of Denmark who had been a New England resident and merchant seaman before coming to California, Jacobs was originally a gold seeker. Like many miners, however, he soon decided there had to be a better way to make a living than standing in cold water shoveling gravel. He bought a small sailing vessel and began hauling cargoes on the bay. Jacobs's decision in 1853 to base his operations on what was to become the Berkeley waterfront was certainly linked to Domingo Peralta's land sales during the same year. As the rancho property was transformed into cropland, the area's new farmers desperately needed access to markets, and Jacobs's vessel provided it. In 1854 he built a small wharf, inevitably called

Jacobs's Landing, which became the hub of the new community's commerce.

Also in 1854, another former merchant seaman, Captain William Bowen, opened an inn on Contra Costa Road, a wagon and stage route that extended north to south along the East Bay shoreline. Because the alignment paralleled the old trail to the Castro family's Rancho San Pablo, locals informally called the thoroughfare "San Pablo Road." Eventually it became San Pablo Avenue. Bowen initially served food and drink and soon added a general store for the convenience of the growing number of farm families in the region. His inn was thus Berkeley's first retail establishment. If Contra Costa Road–San Pablo Avenue was Berkeley's first north-south street, the well-worn trail between Bowen's Inn and Jacobs's Landing, roughly today's Delaware Street, might qualify as the city's first east-west boulevard. A building that may well be Bowen's original inn still stands in the Delaware Street historic district.

In 1855 Ocean View got its first manufacturing plant, the Pioneer Starch and Grist Mill, owned by John Everding and A. A. Rammelsburg. By the midfifties, San Francisco was developing an industrial base, but entrepreneurs like Everding and Rammelsburg were already seeking out suburban locations with cheap land and abundant water. The owners of the Pioneer Mill found these on the Berkeley waterfront, and Jacobs's wharf provided access to regional markets. In addition, Ocean View area grain farmers were able to supply the mill's raw material. Rammelsburg soon sold his share of the business to Everding, but both men were important figures in the local economy for many years to come. Everding's son-in-law, John Schmidt, farmed a portion of Domingo Peralta's old homestead for decades: the land was still in agricultural production in the 1920s. The Pioneer Mill structure, built from redwood cut in the Oakland hills, stood for a century, until it was finally demolished by the Truitt and White Lumber Company in the 1950s.

A year after the starch mill began operation, Ocean View got its second industrial enterprise: Z. B. Heywood's lumberyard. A Maine native with experience in the lumber business, Heywood had established a sawmill at Gualala, about a hundred miles north of San Francisco on the Sonoma-Mendocino coast. He needed a Bay Area storage and distribution center and chose Ocean View for some of the same reasons that had attracted Everding and Rammelsburg. Heywood cooperated with Jacobs to improve and extend the Ocean View wharf so that it could handle the high volume of traffic produced by the new enterprise. Extending the wharf farther into the bay was vital, because the water off the Berkeley shore is shallow. Even after Heywood and Jacobs built the pier out 1,300 feet from the shoreline, some vessels still had problems using it at low tide.

Z. B. Heywood had thirteen children, and the large and energetic Heywood clan played an important role in Berkeley life for the next several decades. During the early twentieth century, for example, three different Heywoods served as the city's mayor. One of the Heywood family homes still stands on Fifth Street. The early development of Ocean View thus produced both enterprises that would be key to the economic future of the city and individuals and families who were to be pillars of Berkeley's business and political elite.

The mill and lumberyard workers and their families, along with the residents of nearby farms, made Ocean View a vital community. In 1856 the Ocean View School was established on San Pablo Road, just north of Bowen's Inn. By 1857 an itinerant preacher was serving the village. The 1860 census counted sixty-nine people in Ocean View proper, and the numbers increased gradually during the next decade.

FIGURE 3. Rev. Henry Durant, the president of the College of California and the first president of the new state university, tried to resolve conflicts between Ocean View and the campus community during the 1870s. Bancroft Library, University of California, Berkeley.

In 1873 Ocean View businessmen, including Jacobs and Rammelsburg, joined with the former University of California president Henry Durant to create the Berkeley Land and Town Improvement Association. The association's purpose was to promote the development of West Berkeley, as Ocean View was increasingly coming to be called. The group laid out streets on a grid plan, subsidized a short-lived ferry service to San Francisco, and publicized and promoted their community as a business location. In 1877 the Southern Pacific Railroad located its transcontinental mainline along the Berkeley shore, giving West Berkeley businesses direct access to the national rail network for the first time. As a result of this activity, several new businesses arrived in the 1870s and 80s. Included were what eventually became the Niehaus and Schuster Planing Mill and the Cornell Watch Company, whose giant factory went through several owners and uses before burning to the ground in 1899. R. P. Thomas also moved his Standard Soap Company from San Francisco to West Berkeley in the 1870s. The company was eventually bought by Colgate-Palmolive, which continued to operate a Berkeley facility until the 1980s.

BLUE-COLLAR TOWN

Ocean View/West Berkeley soon developed into a lively working-class and agricultural community. Most of its residents lived in fairly modest homes scattered among the district's plants, mills, and shops or on farms adjacent to the industrial section. Retail businesses, located on San Pablo Road or lower University Avenue, included several taverns and a beer garden on the site now occupied by Spenger's Fresh Fish Grotto and Restaurant. Between 1880 and 1900, the population grew from a little under 700 to more than 1,500, becoming ever more diverse in the process. Even in the 1850s and 60s, Ocean View boasted substantial national and ethnic diversity, very much reflecting the social mix of people who had originally come to California during the Gold Rush. While the majority of gold seekers were young, English-speaking white men from the eastern and midwestern United States, a significant number were members of immigrant and ethnic minorities. On the day California won statehood in 1850, it already had the most diverse population of any American state.

The Gold Rush occurred in the midst of a large Irish Catholic migration to the United States, stimulated by the great Irish potato famine of 1846–47. Some of Berkeley's earliest farmers were Irish immigrants, including Michael Curtis, James McGee, and John Kearney. The first Catholic religious services were held in Curtis's barn, and McGee eventually donated the land on which the area's first Catholic church and school, St Joseph's, were built. The state located the Asylum for the Deaf, Dumb, and Blind on land bought from Kearney (and now the site of UC Berkeley's Clark Kerr Campus). Two of Curtis's daughters married into the Brennan family, which operated an Ocean View livery stable. The family's name still graces a popular West Berkeley tavern and restaurant.

Irish immigrants also worked in Ocean View's mills and plants, often joined by Scandinavians, Canadians, Mexicans, and Chileans, among others. By the end of the nineteenth century, Germans outnumbered the Irish as the largest foreign-born group, and Italians, Portuguese, and a small population of African Americans had also been added to the mix. Chinese immigrants worked in some of the mills and also operated laundries. Chinese farmers raised fruits and vegetables on small rented plots, selling the products door-to-door. In the early twentieth century, West Berkeley became home to a growing Finnish population, and the Finnish Hall, still located on Tenth Street, is tangible evidence of that once-thriving community. (Actually, there were two Finnish Halls, because the community was deeply split along political lines.) Well into the twentieth century, West Berkeley was an ethnically and nationally mixed, largely working-class neighborhood, much like West Oakland or San Francisco's Mission District. The Murphys lived next door to the Schroeders and across the street from the Garibaldis. Until at least the 1920s, the majority of the population was made up of immigrants and their American-born children.

While urbanization and industrialization were proceeding, much of the Berkeley flatlands remained agricultural. One of the most prominent early farmers was Napoleon Bonaparte Byrne, a Democrat and slave owner from Missouri. Byrne arrived in 1859, accompanied by two former slaves who may have been the area's first African American residents. One of them, Pete Byrne, eventually broke with his former master and became a successful small businessman. Napoleon Byrne farmed nearly a thousand acres in what is now North Berkeley. In 1868 he built the Cedars, an impressive home that survived for nearly 120 years on the Oxford Street site of the Church of the Cedars before being destroyed by fire in the 1980s. (In 2001 the city approved Temple Beth El's proposal for a new synagogue and community center on the same site, though not without considerable neighborhood controversy about the scale of development.) Byrne's Democratic and Confederate political leanings made him something of a pariah in predominantly Republican, Unionist Berkeley. But he was rewarded for his political loyalty in 1885, when the Democratic president, Grover Cleveland, appointed him Berkeley postmaster. By that time, he had sold his home and much of his land to Henry Berryman, a major force in Berkeley development in the late nineteenth century. Some of the large conifers originally planted by Byrne still stand in Live Oak Park.

THE COLLEGE OF CALIFORNIA

Byrne's neighbor to the south was Orrin Simmons, still another former seafaring man, who is important in Berkeley history because his farm was destined to become the campus of the University of California. The arrival of the university in 1873 marks Berkeley's second beginning, the creation of an academic community that was destined to become the city's dominant economic and social force.

The origins of the university go back to the convictions and aspirations of two New England Congregationalist ministers, Samuel Hopkins Willey and Henry Durant. Willey arrived in California in 1849, sent by the Home Missionary Society to bring Protestant godliness to the particularly ungodly social environment of Gold Rush California. Almost immediately he began lobbying for the establishment of a Christian college to train new generations of California leaders. His plans didn't come to much until Reverend Durant arrived in 1853. A Yale graduate with great energy and ability, Durant began to transform Willey's ideas into reality. Realizing that before he could found a college he first had to find students capable of college work, in 1853 Durant established Contra Costa Academy, a private secondary school in Oakland. In 1855 Durant and Willey were ready for the next step: the creation of a nondenominational Christian institution of higher education called the College of California, also located in Oakland.

The model for the new institution was the elite private New England college, which provided young gentlemen with a liberal arts education that emphasized classical studies and Christian morality. To remove such students from the temptations of the city and the cares of the day, New England colleges were usually located in rural areas or small towns. Perhaps that is why Willey and Durant chose not to locate their institution in San Francisco. But Oakland also turned out to have drawbacks. A larger and much rowdier version of Ocean View, Oakland in the 1850s was neither removed from temptation nor free of worldly cares. Durant temporarily located the Contra Costa Academy in a former dance hall of dubious reputation. He was shocked to discover that in the

FIGURE 4. Rev. Samuel Hopkins Willey, founder of the College of California, moved to the new Berkeley subdivision in the mid-1860s. Bancroft Library, University of California, Berkeley.

evening the caretakers were continuing to use the building for its earlier "immoral" purposes. The new college was to be located on a lot bounded by Twelfth, Fourteenth, Franklin, and Harrison Streets, but Durant had to resist, sometimes with threats of force, potential squatters and unpaid contractors who attempted to occupy the site. By the time the College of California moved into its new buildings in 1860, Durant and Willey had already chosen another, more suitable location.

As early as 1857, Durant was inspecting Orrin Simmons's land. Located five miles north of Oakland in a bucolic setting, the site commanded a spectacular view of the Golden Gate. Strawberry Creek seemed to offer an adequate water supply, and Simmons was eager to sell. He was apparently a better sailor than farmer and was looking to profit from some judicious land speculation.

By the end of 1857, Durant and Willey had persuaded the members of the college's board of trustees to allocate funds to purchase a portion of Simmons's property. Eventually the college bought the entire farm for thirty-five thousand dollars. (Simmons had originally paid less than five thousand.) In 1860 the trustees joined Willey and Durant at a rocky outcrop for a ceremony dedicating the new campus. That ceremonial site, at the northeast corner of the modern campus, is known as Founders' Rock.

By 1864 the college had obtained some additional parcels adjacent to the Simmons property but had not even begun to accumulate the funds necessary to pay for the move from Oakland. The trustees hoped to remedy that situation by establishing the College Homestead Association, in effect a wholly owned subsidiary which would subdivide and sell the land south of the property specifically reserved for the campus. The expected profits from the land sales would pay for the relocation of the college.

The new community was to be upscale, populated by solid citizens living in the refined atmosphere of a college town. The trustees hired Frederick Law Olmsted, the designer of New York's Central Park, to plan the development, but his ideas turned out to be too radical. He envisioned landscaped roads which followed the contours of the hill, along the lines of the contemporary Piedmont Avenue. Instead the college authorities adopted a traditional grid pattern. In conformance with the presumed intellectual tone of the new community, north-south streets were named in alphabetical order for men of science: Audubon (now College Avenue), Bowditch, Choate (now Telegraph Avenue), Dana, Ellsworth, Fulton, and Guyot (now Shattuck). East-west streets took the names of men of letters: Allston, Bancroft, Channing, and Dwight.

Olmsted suggested that the new community be called Peralta, but the college trustees wanted something more in keeping with the exalted intellectual and social character they envisioned for their development. At the suggestion of the trustee Frederick Billings, they named the community after George Berkeley, an eighteenth-century British philosopher and man of letters and the Anglican bishop of Cloyne, Ireland, who had been a strong supporter of colonial education. What particularly attracted the trustees was a line in one of Berkeley's poems: "Westward the course of empire takes its way." The trustees, a confident group of prosperous, prominent men, were still very much affected by the Manifest Destiny ideology that had promoted the American conquest of California two decades earlier. To them it must have seemed altogether fitting and proper that the Pacific Basin would be the next "course of empire" for American expansion. The idea of a brave new college community overlooking the Golden Gate and the new Pacific frontier was irresistible.

LAND-GRANT UNIVERSITY

The trustees apparently believed that if they simply built their ambitious new community, the people would come. But that wasn't the case. In 1865 Reverend Willey loyally built a new house in the Berkeley development and began planting trees on the campus and along the streets, but for the next few years, he had no neighbors. It looked as if funds to move the college to Berkeley would never be available; indeed, the institution was having difficulty paying its Oakland bills. In 1867, however, an intriguing new possibility was raised when the state legislature voted to establish a state-supported institution of higher learning.

The original state constitution of 1849 had provided for a state university, but little progress was made on the matter until the U.S. Congress passed the Morrill Land Grant College Act of 1862. The law provided for grants of federal lands to states, which could use income from the sale of the property to support the operations of public universities. The new, federally subsidized institutions were to be people's colleges rather than elitist private institutions like the College of California. The land-grant colleges would teach practical courses in agriculture and mechanics as well as traditional liberal arts offerings. In California, the practical side of the program gave the concept of a state university new political support from labor and farm organizations. And the possibility of privatizing two hundred thousand acres of valuable public land in the Central Valley attracted real-estate and agricultural interests. By 1867, the question was no longer whether there was going to be a University of California, but only where it would be located.

In that year, the trustees of the College of California made the state an offer too good to refuse. If the state agreed to maintain the college as the liberal arts section of the new university, the trustees would transfer their institution and its Berkeley and Oakland properties to state control. This arrangement allowed California to create an instant university and continue giving courses at the Oakland site while a new campus was built in Berkeley. The state sold the noncampus properties of the former college to private parties, thus producing more revenues for the new institution. In 1868, John Dwinelle, a prominent lawyer who served both in the legislature and as a trustee of the College of California, guided the Organic Act of the University of California through the legislative process. The law vested authority over the university in a largely autonomous Board of Regents, and not surprisingly Dwinelle was one of the first appointees. The governor signed the act on March 23, 1868, and Berkeleyans knew for sure that the university was coming to town.

In 1869 the College of California was formally transferred to state control, and for the next four years classes continued in Oakland under the interim presidency of Reverend Durant. Regent

FIGURE 5. North Hall, one of the two original university buildings. Its site is now occupied by the Doe Library Annex. Bancroft Library, University of California, Berkeley.

Sam Merritt, a wealthy lumber merchant and Oakland mayor, chaired the building committee and oversaw construction of the new campus. There was a whiff of scandal when it was discovered that the university was buying materials from Merritt's firm, but by 1873 the first two buildings, imaginatively called North Hall and South Hall, were ready for occupancy. North Hall has long since disappeared, making way for the east wing of the Doe Library. But South Hall still stands, handsomely restored as a tangible link to the university's earliest beginnings. In the fall of 1873, the university moved to Berkeley, led by its new president, Daniel Coit Gilman, who proclaimed, "We have come up hither to this house of our expectations."

FIGURE 6. The Telegraph Avenue horsecar line, linking the UC campus with downtown Oakland. It began service in 1873, the same year the university arrived in Berkeley. Bancroft Library, University of California, Berkeley.

CAMPUS COMMUNITY

Whatever those expectations were, the amenities of Berkeley in 1873 didn't match them. Most students and faculty initially chose to live in Oakland, commuting to classes on a horsecar line that proceeded up Telegraph Road and Choate Street to the south entrance of the campus. The car moved so slowly that patrons often walked alongside for variety. Students seeking diversion would lean one way and then the other until they knocked the swaying car off its tracks. Then everyone would get out and lift the vehicle back into place. In 1876 a steam-driven car replaced the horse and presumably speeded up service.

Gradually, along Choate Street immediately south of campus, businesses opened to serve the new community: first a rooming house and French Charley's restaurant (which was reported to charge outrageous prices), then another rooming house and hotel, a grocery, a laundry, and Dr. Merrill's drugstore. Professors and businesspeople began building houses on the old College Homestead Association lots. South of the campus, a new town was finally taking shape.

The town's growth was further stimulated by the presence of another important state institution, which had arrived in Berkeley even before the university. In 1868 the state Asylum for the Deaf, Dumb, and Blind was preparing to move from San Francisco to a new facility under construction a few blocks south of the university campus. On the morning of October 21, work on the project was interrupted by what seismologists today believe was a magnitude 7.0 earthquake on the Hayward Fault. A workman on the roof of the new school said the massive stone structure "swayed back and forth not less than four feet . . . it seemed to be tossing like a ship on a wild sea." The quake dumped cargoes on Jacobs's wharf into the bay and destroyed Domingo Peralta's original adobe. But overall damage in Berkeley was light, in part because there was so little to be damaged. (Oakland, southern Alameda County, and downtown San Francisco suffered much greater damage.) Because of the earthquake, the new university buildings, particularly South Hall, were constructed with elaborate bracing. The Deaf and Blind Asylum sustained some damage, but repairs allowed classes to begin more or less on schedule in 1869.

EAST VERSUS WEST

The community south of campus grew steadily, so that by the time the Peralta land case was finally settled in 1877, what is today Berkeley was occupied by two well-established settlements separated by more than a mile of fields, pastures, and marshlands. But the communities were divided by more than physical space. Ocean View was heavily immigrant, substantially Catholic, and working-class, essentially an industrial and farming town. The campus community, on the other hand, was primarily middle- or upper-middle-class, inhabited by native-born Protestants, many of whom worked in professional occupations.

Along with these social and economic differences, there were some very specific points of conflict. When the university dammed Strawberry Creek for a water supply, Ocean View residents claimed this action substantially lowered the water level in their wells. They also argued that waste from the campus area was polluting the stream. Shortly after the university occupied its new buildings, a delegation of state legislators visited Berkeley and witnessed a group of somewhat wobbly undergraduates returning from a drinking bout in the hills. The result was a law prohibiting the sale of alcoholic beverages within two miles of campus. This would have closed down taverns in Ocean View, a matter of no little concern to that hard-working and often hard-drinking community. The limit was reduced to one mile, but that caused other problems. Soon there were new bars opening in Ocean View catering specifically to students, and Ocean View parents claimed their community was plagued by drunk and disorderly louts from the university who were leading the town youths astray.

Despite these conflicts, however, ties were growing between the communities. Blue-collar workers from Ocean View found construction and maintenance jobs at the university, and the campus community was a valuable market for Ocean View shops, mills, and farms. Residents of both areas realized that problems like law and order and water pollution could be solved only by cooperation. No one tried harder to bring the two communities together than Henry Durant. After his retirement from the university in 1873, he joined the Berkeley Land and Town Improvement Association, which was promoting development in Ocean View. Durant lobbied for a horsecar line down University Avenue to unify the two Berkeleys. However, he had to settle for a stage that made only four trips per day. The horsecar line was not built until 1891, and even today most of Berkeley's main thoroughfares run north-south rather than east-west. Durant also hoped a new Ocean View ferry would provide a shared link to San Francisco. But the service lasted only two years, despite a financial subsidy from R. P. Thomas, owner of the Standard Soap Company.

In 1874 Durant chaired a public meeting to promote the incorporation of a city that would include both communities. But Ocean View opposition, particularly from farmers who feared high property taxes, killed the proposal. Henry Durant died in 1875, but his efforts on behalf of unification were carried on by others. Professor Martin Kellogg chaired another incorporation meeting in 1877 that proved far more successful. Residents from both Berkeleys were dissatisfied with the level of services from the county government, which had jurisdiction over unincorporated areas. Moreover, Oakland seemed to be making plans to extend its borders north to include both the campus and Ocean View. Nothing promotes unity more than a common enemy, and Oakland thus proved an ideal unifying force. The meeting overwhelmingly supported a petition to the state legislature requesting incorporation. The legislature voted its approval, and on April 1, 1878, the governor signed a bill that formally established the city of Berkeley.

Cynics may find it particularly appropriate that a place that is sometimes called "Berserkeley" was incorporated on April Fools' Day. But incorporation was a serious matter. It may have been a shotgun wedding, but two very different communities were now joined together in an uneasy political union that has lasted more than 125 years.

CHAPTER THREE

ENTER THE OCTOPUS

In 1878 the borders of the newly incorporated Berkeley stretched from the bay to the crest of the eastern hills and approximately from what is today Eunice Street on the north boundary to Derby Street on the south. This area included the populated parts of Ocean View and the campus community, but it also contained thousands of acres of open space, including the fields and vacant lands between the two settlements. Incorporation, then, did not end the physical separation between East and West Berkeley, and it also failed to erase the social, cultural, and economic differences between the two communities. If anything, incorporation simply provided an arena in which differences could be aired and battles fought. For the rest of the nineteenth century, the rivalry between east and west was an essential ingredient of Berkeley politics.

Ironically, the Southern Pacific Railroad, the symbol of corporate greed and illegitimate power in late nineteenth-century California, was the force that eventually ameliorated the east-west rivalry by establishing some common ground for the two Berkeleys. In the 1870s, the Southern Pacific was the new name for the

Central Pacific, the company that had received federal subsidies to build the western half of the transcontinental railroad. Construction was completed in 1869, and Oakland became the railroad's western terminus. As a result, Oakland rapidly developed into California's second city and an integral part of the Bay Area's urban core. The railroad, meanwhile, grew into the state's largest corporation and most important economic force. For the rest of the nineteenth century, it dominated many aspects of California life. The author Frank Norris, a former UC Berkeley student, found an apt metaphor for its power in the title of his 1901 novel *The Octopus.*

EAST VERSUS WEST (CONTINUED)

While the railroad consolidated its statewide power, Berkeley organized its new political structure. On May 13, 1878, the community's voters (all male) went to the polls to choose the town's first five-member board of trustees and six-member school board, as well as the new town clerk, treasurer, assessor, constable, and justices of the peace. Like Berkeley elections in the 1970s, 80s, and 90s, the 1878 contest was dominated by two opposing slates of candidates that reflected the town's east-west split. Middle-class East Berkeley by and large supported the Citizen's Ticket, while much of working-class West Berkeley rallied around the Workingman's Party. When the three-hundred-odd votes were tallied, the Workingmen had won a significant victory, produced in part by an effective last-minute get-out-the-vote campaign. (The Workingman's winning slate included a few candidates, like the school board member Martin Kellogg, who were also endorsed by the Citizen's Ticket.)

The Citizen's Ticket reflected local Berkeley political interests, but the Workingman's Party was a statewide organization. Established in 1877 by San Francisco labor activists, the party was a political response to the economic depression of the 1870s. Although its platform included progressive reforms like the eight-hour working day and greater educational opportunities for working-class children, by 1878 the organization was dominated by Denis Kearney and his demagogic politics of anti-Chinese racism. Kearney ignored the complex causes of the depression, blaming virtually all of California's problems on the presence of Chinese immigrants. His huge sandlot rallies in San Francisco ended with the chant "The Chinese must go!"

Although the Berkeley election was fought mainly on local issues, anti-Chinese activity was very much a part of the community's social landscape. A "Chinese Must Go" rally was held on Shattuck Avenue, and several Chinese businesses were vandalized. In at least one instance, a Chinese man drew a gun to defend himself against a gang of white youths. The Workingman's Party eventually self-destructed as prosperity returned in the early 1880s, but anti-Asian prejudice continued to be an almost institutionalized part of both California and Berkeley life.

On the local level, the results of the 1878 election represented a substantial victory for West Berkeley and marked the beginning of several decades of sectional conflict in Berkeley politics. The town trustees were originally chosen at large, with all voters electing all trustees. In 1895, Berkeley switched to a ward system, dividing the city into wards, with a representative elected by each ward. In part the change reflected West Berkeley's realization that, as the years had passed, the eastern section of the city had steadily gained population, influence, and power. The ward system at least guaranteed West Berkeleyans some representation on the board of trustees.

Even something as seemingly trivial as the location of the post office became an emotional east-west issue. When federal authorities determined that the facility would be in Ocean View rather than the university community, university administrators refused to patronize it, transporting the UC mail all the way to San Francisco to avoid benefiting West Berkeley. Eventually the authorities resolved the conflict by establishing post office branches in both areas.

Another matter that continued to divide Berkeleyans was the sale and consumption of alcoholic beverages. The campus community had an active chapter of the Women's Christian Temperance Union, which championed the prohibition of alcohol as an issue of Christian morality and a means to protect women and children from poverty and domestic abuse. The WCTU also served as an avenue for middle-class women to become involved in broader political and community issues. Its strongest support came from respectable East Berkeleyans and the most vehement opposition from West Berkeley tavern owners and brewery operators. The city trustees outlawed the sale of booze in 1899 but rescinded the action a year later. In 1906 the measure was reinstated, and Berkeley remained officially dry until national prohibition was overturned in 1933. Unofficially, however, some West Berkeley cafes and South Campus student hangouts continued to be more than a little bit damp. Willard Middle School, named after a national leader of the WCTU, reflects the influence that the antialcohol crusade had on Berkeley life and culture.

The east-west rivalry also affected proceedings of the school board. At the time of Berkeley's incorporation, the Ocean View School had been serving West Berkeley for more than twenty years. Kellogg School, named after the UC professor who was then the school board president, opened in 1880 to serve the campus community. Both institutions went up only to the eighth grade, and many well-educated East Berkeley parents requested the establishment of a high school for their children. This demand was partially met by a number of private academies, including an institution run by Anna Head, one of the first women graduates of the university. (The current Head-Royce School in Oakland traces its origins back to the original Anna Head School, established on Channing Way in the 1880s.)

But these private institutions in no way diminished East Berkeley's campaign for a public high school. Most middle-class parents expected the school to be located near the campus, but working-class West Berkeleyans opposed the establishment of a high school outside their community that would serve few of their children (most of whom left school after the eighth grade). In 1882 the school board approved a compromise that allowed high-school-level courses to be taught at the Kellogg site, but a bond issue to build a separate high school did not pass until 1900. Even then, the bond met with substantial West Berkeley opposition.

Given these sectional and class conflicts, town officials were understandably nervous about the location of government operations. The trustees avoided building a town hall for six years, holding their meetings in rented facilities alternately in East and West Berkeley. In 1884 they finally bit the bullet, deciding to locate the hall at roughly the corner of today's University Avenue and Sacramento Street. This put the seat of local government pretty much in the middle of nowhere, surrounded by open fields and pastures. The site's one virtue was that it was equally inconvenient for residents of both communities. Each could at least be satisfied that its rival had not been favored with the town hall.

COMMON GROUND

By the end of the nineteenth century, the Southern Pacific Railroad's Berkeley branch line finally created the common ground that served as the logical location for most of the city's public institutions. In 1877 the railroad relocated its main line along the Berkeley waterfront, where it remains today (now under Union Pacific ownership). This change contributed to the commercial and industrial development of West Berkeley, but the railroad did not provide regular Berkeley passenger service until the twentieth century. (And the Santa Fe Railroad did not build into Berkeley until 1902.) If nineteenth-century Berkeley was going to be integrated into the regional and national rail network, it needed a local branch line linking the town with the SP's West Oakland depot and ferry terminal, which provided service to San Francisco.

Such a branch line was Francis Kittredge Shattuck's earnest hope and vision. We have already seen that Shattuck, along with his brother-in-law George Blake and partners William Hillegass and James Leonard, was one of the town's original Anglo landowners (and illegal squatters on Domingo Peralta's land). For many years, Shattuck, Blake, and Hillegass lived in Oakland, while Leonard farmed the partners' Berkeley property. Shattuck became an important business and political figure in Oakland, serving as mayor, city councilor, and county supervisor. In 1868, however, he moved to Berkeley, building an impressive house with elaborate gardens on the site of today's Shattuck Plaza Hotel. He sold a plot of forty acres south of his home to the San Francisco hardware merchant J. L. Barker, and in the 1870s the two men worked together to develop their properties. Their most ambitious scheme was to persuade the Southern Pacific to build a local line through the Shattuck and Barker land holdings. They offered to provide a free Berkeley right-of-way, twenty additional acres for a station and rail yard, and a twenty-thousand-dollar cash subsidy. The offer was sufficient to persuade the Southern Pacific to form a separate corporation, the Western Development Company, to build a local line to Berkeley.

The line followed a route that today includes Stanford Avenue (named after the railroad president Leland Stanford), Adeline Street, and Shattuck Avenue. The odd angle of Adeline in South Berkeley is the result of the alignment of the original rail right-of-way. At University Avenue, the route looped back so that the train could return to Oakland on the original single track. Inside that loop, now Shattuck Square, the railroad built its Berkeley station. That general location has been Berkeley's transit hub ever since. The Downtown Berkeley BART station is just a few yards southwest of the original branch-line depot, and the AC Transit F bus still follows much of the original branch-line route. The tracks to University Avenue were completed in 1876. In 1878 they were extended north to Vine Street, encouraging the initial commercial and residential development of what today is the North Shattuck neighborhood (also known as the Gourmet Ghetto).

The branch line was the most convenient route to Oakland and the Southern Pacific ferry to San Francisco for both East and West Berkeley. It provided faster and more efficient service than either the San Pablo Avenue stage or the Telegraph Road steam streetcar. As Shattuck and Barker had fervently hoped, the railroad eventually made Shattuck Avenue, between University Avenue and Dwight Way, into Berkeley's downtown, a prosperous central commercial district serving both East and West Berkeley.

In a sense, then, the Shattuck Avenue corridor became common ground for Berkeley's rival sections. By the turn of the century, it was logical that Berkeley's major civic buildings and institutions be located there. In 1899, the town hall was put on wheels and moved to a site on Grove Street (now Martin Luther King Jr. Way) between Allston Way and Center Street, just two blocks west of Shattuck. When the modest wooden building burned down in 1904, it was replaced by the current Old City Hall, completed in 1909 and now the headquarters of the Berkeley Unified School District. In 1901, after a school bond issue

FIGURE 7. The "new" Berkeley City Hall, constructed in 1909 and seen here in the 1920s. Bancroft Library, University of California, Berkeley.

finally passed, the city built the long-awaited high school on Milvia Street, one block west of Shattuck. The public library was located on Shattuck itself, as was the main post office (until 1914, when a new building was built on Allston Way, one block west). But if the branch line brought Berkeleyans together, it also created a visible dividing line. By the turn of the century, Berkeley already had a right (east) and wrong (west) side of the tracks.

MOVERS AND SHAKERS

Francis Kittredge Shattuck certainly deserves consideration as Berkeley's most important mover and shaker during the late nineteenth century. In addition to conducting his development and real-estate activities, he served as president of the town's first bank, established in 1891. In the same year, Shattuck provided a small site for Berkeley's first public library and agreed to serve as president of its board of trustees. His wife, Rosa M. Shattuck, donated a larger site for a library constructed with Carnegie Foundation funds fourteen years later. That structure housed the library until the current Shattuck Avenue location was occupied in 1931.

Many other Berkeleyans played prominent roles in the community's nineteenth-century development. (Mark) Ashby Avenue and (William) Woolsey and (Noah) Webster streets are examples of thoroughfares named for prominent nineteenth-century settlers who subdivided their properties and promoted residential growth. Edward Harmon was one of several Berkeley farmers who became land developers. Most simply subdivided and platted property, selling lots to homeowners or contractors who built homes on speculation. Harmon, however, went into the construction business himself and over a twenty-year period built more than forty houses on what had previously been his South Berkeley farmland. He was the major developer of the unincorporated community of Lorin, which once boasted a train station at Adeline Street and Alcatraz Avenue, as well as a school and post office. In the early 1890s, Berkeley annexed Lorin and some adjacent tracts in the city's first territorial expansion.

Henry Berryman was North Berkeley's leading nineteenth-century developer. A wealthy coal merchant and importer, Berryman bought Napoleon Bonaparte Byrne's farm in 1870 and moved into the Cedars, the large home Byrne had built two years earlier. Berryman subdivided the farm and became so prominent in North Berkeley life that when the Southern Pacific extended its branch line to Vine Street, the new depot became known as Berryman Station. He and his business associate, Felix Chappellet, bought the original waterworks established by the College of California. They extended the pipes, offering service to individual homeowners. (Although Chappellet was unusual among pioneer Berkeley developers in not naming a street for himself, he did so honor his wife, Milvia.) In 1877 Berryman bought out his partner's interest in the water company and built Berryman Reservoir on Codornices Creek. Five years later, Berryman himself sold out, and Berkeley's water works were integrated into a larger East Bay system.

The most unusual nineteenth-century Berkeley developer was Maurice Strellinger, also known as Maurice Curtis. Strellinger was a well-known San Francisco comic actor whose play *Sam'l of Posen* was so popular that he became a wealthy man. In the 1880s, he invested in Berkeley real estate, buying considerable acreage in what had once been Domingo Peralta's homestead in north-central Berkeley. Strellinger called his development Peralta Park and marketed it as an exclusive suburban tract where families would enjoy gracious country living. Today, such a development would be sited around a golf course, but in the 1880s such homes were anchored by luxury hotels. In 1888 Strellinger began building the Peralta Park Hotel, a turreted Victorian monstrosity that featured sixty rooms and twenty baths. The hotel opened in 1891, by which time Strellinger had promoted a horsecar line on Sacramento Street north from University Avenue to serve his new neighborhood. He named one Peralta Park street after his dramatic character, Posen, and another for his wife and leading lady, Albina.

In 1892 Strellinger was arrested in San Francisco for drunken behavior after a night of partying. Somehow the arresting officer was shot dead. Strellinger denied any responsibility, but the authorities indicted him for murder. The case went through four trials, two hung juries, and one procedural dismissal. Finally, Strellinger was found not guilty, but he had long since used up his money and most of his public goodwill on his defense. He had to liquidate

FIGURE 8. The gaudy Peralta Park Hotel, built in 1888 by actor Maurice Strellinger, aka Maurice Curtis, aka Sam'l of Posen. Photo courtesy of the Albany Library Historical Photograph Collection, Alameda County Libraries.

his properties, and the hotel went through a number of institutional uses before becoming St. Mary's High School, operated by the Christian Brothers order. The institution still occupies the site, though fire destroyed the turreted upper stories of the old hotel in 1946, and the rest of the building was replaced in 1959. But the Leuders House, the largest of the thirteen Victorian homes built by Strellinger in Peralta Park, still stands on Albina Avenue.

INFRASTRUCTURE

Before his downfall, Maurice Strellinger was also president of the Berkeley Electric Light Company, an enterprise that installed ten electric street lights on high towers and masts in 1888. One wag claimed they only let citizens see how dark it was, but the town agreed to buy the system from its private subscribers and operated the street lights for three years. When individual homeowners began signing up for electricity service in 1891, the town privatized the operation, selling the enterprise back to individual investors. Eventually, Berkeley's electricity system was integrated into the Pacific Gas and Electric Company's regional monopoly, though the idea of a municipally owned system for Berkeley, like those operating in Alameda and Palo Alto, never completely died. Reformers proposed public power for Berkeley in the early twentieth century and again in the 1980s. A statewide power crisis in 2001 prompted further discussion, and the city council agreed to study the matter once again.

Telephone service came to Berkeley in 1882 (through two separate, unconnected systems). The first coal-gas lines were laid in Ocean View in 1877 and extended to East Berkeley in the early 1880s. Berkeley also got its first volunteer fire departments in the early eighties. The very first was the Tiger in West Berkeley, established in 1882, but it was unable to prevent the Brennan brothers' livery stable from going up in flames in 1883. Soon afterward, East Berkeley also established a fire station, the Columbia, and in 1887 the ubiquitous Maurice Strellinger subsidized the Posen Chemical Number One in his Peralta Park development. In 1891 South Berkeley got its very own Peralta Hook and Ladder Company. When they weren't fighting fires, the volunteer departments served as important community institutions, connecting Berkeley men of various social backgrounds in significant economic and political networks.

PHYSICAL TRANSFORMATION

The growth of Berkeley during the railroad age—the new homes, businesses, and infrastructure—profoundly changed the area's physical environment. In the 1850s and 60s, much of the former Peralta rancho was transformed from pasture to cultivated farmland. By the 1880s, however, substantial housing tracts and business districts were encroaching on the farms. Developers began filling marshes, channeling creeks into culverts, and destroying riparian vegetation. Although Berkeleyans waxed poetic about their "Mediterranean" environment, they were transforming it into a landscape that looked suspiciously like the eastern United States. Homeowners planted lawns and all manner of flowers and shrubs imported from the east. During the dry Mediterranean-style summers, such gardens demanded prodigious amounts of scarce water.

Most of all, Berkeleyans, like many other nineteenth-century Americans, planted trees, a process which in Berkeley transformed bald grasslands into a substantial urban forest. As we have seen, Samuel Hopkins Willey was an inveterate tree planter, and many generations of Berkeley residents and campus planners followed in his footsteps, with dramatic results. In 1878 the owner of the Dwight Way Nursery claimed that he had already sold fifty thousand trees to the residents of the new town. J. L. Barker was just one of many prominent Berkeley businessmen who promoted the annual celebration of Arbor Day with mass tree plantings. Virtually all the species planted were nonnative. Even the coast redwood and Monterey pine that form such a handsome part of Berkeley's landscape today were native to nearby areas but not to Berkeley itself. The ubiquitous blue gum eucalyptus was introduced into California from Australia in the 1850s, and Berkeley tree enthusiasts planted it with abandon. The eucalyptus grove near the west gate of the campus, planted as a windbreak in the 1870s, contains some of the oldest and tallest examples of the species in the Bay Area and perhaps the United States. Cedar Street may have been named for a large West Berkeley conifer planted more than a century ago. In 1998, El Niño–driven storms toppled the tree (which was actually a cypress), killing a passing motorist in a bizarre, unintentional consequence of one nineteenth-century attempt at beautification.

These changes in the landscape are some of the most dramatic reflections of Berkeley's substantial economic and population growth during California's railroad age, the age of the Octopus. Berkeley's population increased from fewer than two thousand residents in 1878 to more than thirteen thousand in 1900. But the community's movers and shakers believed this was just the beginning, and they were right. At the dawn of the new century, Berkeley was embarking on the greatest economic and population boom in its history—one that would transform a still-rural town into a city.

CHAPTER FOUR

URBANIZATION

In 1900 most Berkeley streets were unpaved, many homes were still not hooked up to water and sewer lines, and there were still indeed farms in Berkeley. During the next two decades, however, the town became a city as a result of tremendous economic and population growth. From 13,214 residents in 1900, Berkeley's population increased to 56,036 in 1920. Most of that growth occurred between 1900 and 1910, when the population more than tripled to 40,434. During that decade, Berkeley was the fourth fastest-growing city in the United States, and by 1910 it was the fifth largest city in California. What Malcolm Margolin has called the town's "Bucolic Age" was over, and urbanization was well under way. The Berkeley of 1920 in many ways had more in common with today's urban community than it had with the quiet town of 1900.

EARTHQUAKE COUNTRY

One of the major contributors to growth was the 1906 earthquake. Berkeley, like most of California, is earthquake country. The

Hayward Fault zone runs along the base of the eastern hills, bisecting the university's Memorial Stadium, passing under Bowles and Stern halls and the Greek Theater, and heading north through the North Gate, Cragmont, Northbrae, and Thousand Oaks neighborhoods. The last significant quake on the fault was in 1868. As we have seen, it did little damage in Berkeley because there was so little to be damaged. Seismologists estimate that there is about a 30 per cent chance of a similar, magnitude 7.0 earthquake occurring on the Hayward Fault in or near Berkeley in the next thirty years. This time there will be plenty of destruction, including the possible collapse of several unsafe buildings on campus, damage to unreinforced masonry structures on Telegraph and Shattuck avenues, and threats to homes built on slide areas in the hills and filled-in creeks and marshes in the flatlands. In 1998 the UC chancellor, Robert Berdahl, announced that necessary seismic retrofitting on campus buildings would cost $1 billion.

The 1906 earthquake, however, occurred on the San Andreas Fault, on the west side of the bay. At magnitude 8.0, it was far stronger than any quake predicted for the Hayward Fault. Its greatest impact was on north, south, and west bay communities, including, of course, San Francisco itself. The earthquake and subsequent fire devastated the city, forcing half of its four hundred thousand residents out of their homes at least temporarily and leaving tens of thousands as long-term refugees. By comparison, the impact on the East Bay, including Berkeley, was minor. One source estimated that five thousand Berkeley chimneys collapsed, and most others were damaged, including the large stack of the Standard Soap factory in West Berkeley. Berkeley High had to close for a few months because of cracked walls, and several commercial structures, such as the new Barker Building on Shattuck Avenue, suffered visible damage. The university, however, came through virtually unscathed, and the University Cadet Corps, an early version of the ROTC, was assigned guard duty in San Francisco. On the whole, urban life in Berkeley was able to go on more or less normally after the quake.

With relatively little earthquake damage of their own to repair, Berkeley and other East Bay cities were able to take in tens of thousands of San Francisco refugees. The Southern Pacific gave free ferry and train passage to people leaving the devastated city, and between ten and fifteen thousand took advantage of this transport to come to Berkeley. Many stayed with family and friends, but several thousand were put up in temporary shelters and in camps on the UC campus. Included were refugees from San Francisco's Chinatown, which had been completely destroyed. The *Berkeley Daily Gazette* described a Chinese establishment on Dwight Way that had previously been raided by the police as "a notorious gambling den." Now it served as a nursery for refugee children from Chinatown, in which "more than forty babies from two weeks old to six years are safely housed and cared for." Berkeley mayor Francis Ferrier appointed a City Relief Committee, but after about two weeks the army assumed formal control of the relief effort.

Many of the refugees eventually returned to San Francisco or settled in other communities, but thousands stayed in Berkeley, moving into new housing constructed in the post-earthquake building boom. The city issued 1,283 building permits in 1906, nearly twice as many as in the previous year. Much of the new housing was built in the central section of town, finally filling in the open space that for so long had separated East and West Berkeley.

The earthquake also promoted the relocation of businesses to Berkeley from San Francisco's damaged industrial and commercial districts. "It is not Christian to seek advantage in another's misfortune," one Berkeleyan commented, "but there is nothing to be ashamed of in profiting from such misfortune if it comes

FIGURE 9. 1906 earthquake refugee camp, California Field on the Cal campus. Bancroft Library, University of California, Berkeley.

unsought." And profit Berkeley did. A writer for *Sunset* magazine said it gave observers "a queer and creepy feeling down the spine to drive along the streets of commercial Berkeley and contemplate the business signs" of former San Francisco establishments. In the four months following the earthquake, thirty-seven new factories were built in Berkeley. Between 1906 and 1907, bank deposits in the city increased by 113 percent.

THE KEY SYSTEM

The earthquake was by no means the only reason for the dramatic population and economic growth of the early twentieth century. Berkeley and the rest of the urbanized East Bay developed new transit systems that would have promoted dramatic development during those years even without the quake. Southern Pacific steam trains were important in Berkeley's late nineteenth-century history; in 1891 they were joined by electric rail systems, the latest idea in urban transit. The first successful trolley system was a line from Oakland north along Grove Street (now Martin Luther King Jr. Way) to downtown Berkeley and the UC campus. The Grove Street line was an immediate success and stimulated the construction of additional East Bay systems. By 1893 an effort was already under way to consolidate the separate lines into a single, integrated electric rail system that would eventually cover the entire urban East Bay.

The chief consolidators were Francis "Borax" Smith and Frank Havens. Smith had already made a substantial fortune operating borax mines in southeastern California. He built a large estate in Oakland and was looking for new investment opportunities. Havens, a San Francisco lawyer, had a particular talent for spending Smith's money, and together they made a well-matched, if not entirely successful, team. In 1893 they formed a company called Oakland Transit Consolidated, which not only bought up existing streetcar franchises but also built new lines and integrated them into a unified rail network. The small streetcars became feeders for fast "interurban" trains that linked East Bay cities.

The partners planned to compete head-on with the Southern Pacific ferry service to San Francisco, Smith even contemplating a transit tube under the bay three-quarters of a century before BART actually built one. In the meantime, he had to be content with filling a significant piece of the Emeryville waterfront to create a new ferry terminal (near the present site of the Bay Bridge toll plaza). The Key System, as the new rail line came to be called, introduced fast, propeller-driven ferries on the bay to compete with the slower Southern Pacific paddle-wheel craft.

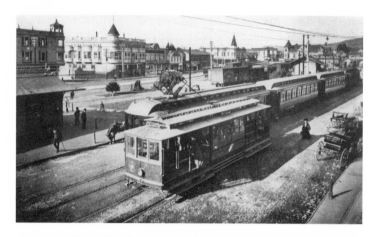

FIGURE 10. Large Key System interurban train with smaller feeder street-car, Shattuck Avenue, downtown Berkeley, 1907. Bancroft Library, University of California, Berkeley.

The Key System was part of a larger Smith-Havens business empire that included the Realty Syndicate, a huge land company that bought and developed thousands of acres of East Bay residential properties. Much of the land was in the hills, including parts of Montclair and Piedmont. In Berkeley, syndicate holdings included significant pieces of the Claremont and Northbrae districts. The syndicate also planned development of the Thousand Oaks neighborhood, in spite of many residents' wish to preserve the area as parkland. The business plan was to extend the electric rails to the syndicate's undeveloped lands, allowing the property to be subdivided for urban and suburban purposes and thus substantially raising its value. Eventually the whole corporate structure was placed under the control of United Properties, a giant holding company whose major investors included the prominent Berkeley developer John Spring. Smith, Havens, and Spring were the instigators of the luxurious Claremont Hotel, on which construction began in 1906. But by the time the hotel opened in 1915, the Smith-Havens empire had crashed and become mired in complex bankruptcy proceedings. This setback didn't stop Smith from starting all over again and making another fortune. Meanwhile, the Key System survived under various ownership structures, lasting until the establishment of the publicly owned AC Transit agency in 1959.

The Key System's interurban mainline reached the downtown Berkeley station on Shattuck Avenue in 1903. Offering thirty-six-minute service to San Francisco via the Emeryville ferry, the trains initially ran once an hour. The route was so popular that service was soon increased to once every twenty minutes. The line eventually extended north to the Northbrae and Thousand Oaks neighborhoods and west to the Westbrae district. In southeast Berkeley, a Key System line up Claremont Avenue promoted the development of the Claremont district and the Claremont Hotel. Smaller, feeder streetcar lines also stimulated the growth of several additional neighborhoods, including the Northside hills and the north campus business district along Euclid Avenue. Similarly, the College Avenue line promoted the development of the Elmwood district and established what is today one of Berkeley's most beloved and protected shopping areas, along College Avenue.

Competition from the Key System forced the Southern Pacific to electrify its branch line in 1911. Now the SP red cars and the Key System orange trains ran virtually side by side on Shattuck Avenue. The Southern Pacific extended its electric line north through the Henry Street tunnel to Solano Avenue and along California Street to the old Peralta Park district. Like the Key System, the SP developed its own network of streetcar feeder lines that in turn promoted the development of additional subdivisions. Inevitably, the city annexed these new neighborhoods: the Claremont district in 1906, portions of Northbrae in 1908, and the rest of Northbrae, as well as Cragmont, Thousand Oaks, and Westbrae, in 1920.

The new rail systems made it practical for many of the new residents of these areas to commute to work in Oakland and San Francisco. The fast electric lines thus allowed Berkeley to function in part as a suburban bedroom community. Berkeley society was becoming more complicated as growing numbers of suburban commuters and their families were added to the mix of West Berkeley workers, downtown business and commercial interests, and university students and professionals.

THE GREAT STATE U

The final reason for Berkeley's dramatic early twentieth-century development was the evolution and growth of the University of California. In the first two decades of the twentieth century, UC not only increased the size of its student body and faculty but also transformed itself into one of the nation's most distinguished universities. To fully understand this transformation, we need to go back to the university's origins. At the time of its founding in 1868, there were two primary models for American higher education: the classical liberal arts college and the new land-grant university, which included practical education in "agriculture and mechanics." With its dual origins as the private College of California and the state's land-grant university, Cal, of course, embodied both these traditions.

In 1872 another model of higher education arrived in California with the coming of the new university president, Daniel Coit Gilman. Gilman was a member of a generation of American educators who admired the German university, with its emphasis on seeking new truths and knowledge through research and the application of the scientific method. Gilman had pioneered this approach as director of the Sheffield School of Science at Yale. He believed that the new community of Berkeley, on the edge of a new American Pacific frontier, was the ideal place to promote and develop a new research-oriented American university. Gilman claimed to have no quarrel with the traditional liberal arts curriculum, but he wished to add more modern subjects of study, particularly in science. He also counted himself a supporter of the land-grant-college concept, but, for him, "agriculture and mechanics" meant not vocational training but the latest research in agronomy and engineering.

Gilman was an articulate, able leader, and he got the university off to a flying start. He persuaded Hugh Toland to donate his San Francisco medical school to the university and received James Lick's bequest for an observatory on Mount Hamilton in Santa Clara County. Gilman established the Berkeley Club to maintain connections between the university and prominent Bay Area citizens. He used such contacts to attract private donations that eventually led to the building of the original, octagonal Harmon Gymnasium and Bacon Hall, housing the university library and art gallery.

But Gilman's educational philosophy came under sharp scrutiny. Conservatives attacked it as godless, while populists criticized it as elitist. The populist challenge was particularly strong, given the social upheaval of the 1870s. Organizations representing labor and small farmers called for the abolition of the Board of Regents and advocated putting the university under the authority of the State Board of Education and the elected superintendent of public instruction. The populist critics had an important ally within the university: the agriculture professor Ezra Carr, who pushed for practical, vocational programs for farmers. Carr had plenty of time to make his views known around the state: in 1873 he had only one student studying his agriculture curriculum.

The debate over the university, its program, and its structure came to a head during a series of legislative hearings in 1874. Gilman offered a masterful defense of his policies, and the legislature declined to tamper with the authority of the Regents. Gilman persuaded the Board of Regents to fire Professor Carr, but Carr managed to get himself elected state superintendent of public instruction and thus became an ex officio member of the very board that had just dismissed him. Nevertheless, the result of the legislative inquiry was a major victory for Gilman. On campus, Carr was eventually succeeded by Eugene Hilgard, who did exactly the kind of rigorous research in agricultural science that Gilman had advocated. But Gilman's supporters had little time to savor their triumph. Their hero was offered the presidency of the new Johns Hopkins University in Baltimore and accepted in late 1874. At Johns Hopkins, Gilman built the kind of research university he had hoped to create in Berkeley.

During the decade and a half following Gilman's departure, UC suffered through a series of generally weak presidents, who were often plagued by interfering Regents, rebellious faculty, and rowdy students. Student disorders, from drunken battles during the annual "Frosh-Soph Rush" to food riots in the North Hall dining room, upset Berkeley residents and kept the town marshal busy. The university thus did little to attract either public support or legislative confidence, and the result was declining enrollments and inadequate funding. Some professors, like the LeConte brothers, John and Joseph, gained formidable reputations, but the institution as a whole had little prestige. In the 1880s, the Southern Pacific Railroad magnate Leland Stanford considered giving the university a sizable donation in memory of his late, beloved son, but the depressing state of the institution, combined with the legislature's refusal to ratify his ap-

FIGURE 11. Longtime Cal professor Martin Kellogg served as university president and brought much-needed stability to the institution in the 1890s. Bancroft Library, University of California, Berkeley.

pointment as Regent, persuaded Stanford to start his own university in Palo Alto instead.

Things began looking up on the Berkeley campus during the 1890s. The presidency of Martin Kellogg finally brought some administrative stability to the institution. A veteran English professor who had long been active in Berkeley civic affairs, Kellogg had sufficient faculty, Regent, and community contacts to gain acceptance, if not always support. The university also benefited from the educational demands of the nation's emerging industrial economy. In Gold Rush California, for example, mining had been an individual adventure, and most miners were untrained amateurs. By the 1890s, mining had become a major corporate industry that needed university-trained engineers, geologists, and managers. Cal was expected to meet those needs as well as similar demands from other industries and professions for university graduates. The legislature passed a statewide property tax of 1 cent per $1,000 assessed valuation for university funding, and enrollment began climbing—from slightly more than two hundred in the early 1880s to nearly two thousand by 1900.

THE HEARST-WHEELER ERA

The most important campus development during the Kellogg years was the growing influence and support of Phoebe Apperson Hearst. The widow of the mining magnate and former United States senator George Hearst, and doting mother of the future media mogul William Randolph Hearst, Phoebe Hearst was a formidable figure in her own right. She had been a teacher before her marriage and took a lifelong interest in education and scholarship. After her husband's death, she used her very great wealth and influence to promote various educational institutions and causes. She was a major supporter of the kindergarten movement, helped establish the Parent-Teacher Association, and sponsored schools for poor children. But most of all she supported and promoted the growth and development of the University of California. She donated funds for a number of projects, including the Hearst Mining Building, the establishment of an anthropology department, and numerous archaeological expeditions. An advocate of female education and suffrage, she was responsible for building a women's gymnasium and establishing scholarships for women students (which inevitably became known as "Phoebes").

Hearst interfered shamelessly, if benevolently, in the lives of the Phoebe recipients. One of her protégés was Julia Morgan, the first female graduate of the mechanical engineering program. Hearst paid Morgan's way through the École des Beaux-Arts in Paris, then considered the world's finest architecture school. For most of her distinguished architectural career, Morgan was associated with Hearst family projects, including the San Simeon castle. Phoebe Hearst maintained a Berkeley home and was usually in residence for a portion of each year to keep a close eye on "her" university. It is entirely appropriate that Hearst Avenue, just north of the Berkeley campus, is named not for the senator or newspaper publisher but for the university's greatest patron, Phoebe Apperson Hearst.

Of all her activities on behalf of UC, none was more important than her role in promoting a master plan for the campus. In 1896, at the suggestion of the architect and mathematics instructor Bernard Maybeck, she donated funds to support an international competition for the development of such a plan. The contest was significant because it committed the university to a policy of extensive expansion and brought Berkeley and the university widespread national and international attention. The French architect Émile Bernard won the ten-thousand-dollar prize, but after he declined to come to Berkeley for the extended period necessary, the university persuaded another contestant, John Galen Howard, to supervise the implementation of the plan.

Howard, who served as university architect until 1924, drastically scaled down Bernard's proposal, in effect creating a Howard Plan that governed the university's physical expansion for more than a quarter of a century. While preserving much of Strawberry

FIGURE 12. Probably the two most influential people in the history of the university, Phoebe Apperson Hearst and Benjamin Ide Wheeler, at commencement exercises, 1913. Bancroft Library, University of California, Berkeley.

Creek and the campus's open space, Howard also designed many of the structures that remain the university's most familiar and impressive landmarks, including Wheeler Hall, Doe Library, Memorial Stadium, Sather Gate, the Hearst Greek Theater, and the Campanile. The architectural historian Loren Partridge argues that "the core of the Berkeley campus by John Galen Howard is one of the largest, most complete Beaux-Arts ensembles ever to be executed in permanent materials in the history of American architecture."

Not surprisingly, Phoebe Hearst was the first female member of the Board of Regents, and she was on the board in 1899 when it chose Benjamin Ide Wheeler as the new university president. A former German and classics professor from Cornell, Wheeler was the first strong president since Daniel Coit Gilman, and he presided over the university for the next twenty years. Like David Starr Jordan, his counterpart at Stanford, Wheeler became an influential figure in Bay Area life. His advice and opinion were sought on matters of culture and public policy, and he served on a number of blue-ribbon committees and advisory boards. With this prestige, he was able to expand the university's financial base, securing increased state funding and persuading other wealthy individuals to follow Phoebe Hearst's example. Jane Sather, for instance, contributed funds both for Sather Gate, in honor of her late husband Peder, and the Sather Tower (the Campanile), as her own personal memorial.

Although he attacked student fraternities as undemocratic, Wheeler was himself personally autocratic, often overriding long-established faculty prerogatives in pursuit of his ambitious goals. Nevertheless, he turned most matters of student discipline over to the students themselves, instituting an honor code for exams and strengthening student government. He strongly supported university athletics but, objecting to football's violence and commercialism, banned the game in favor of rugby for some years before and during World War I.

Most important of all, Wheeler expanded programs and recruited promising young faculty members (often from Ivy League universities). In the process, he went a long way toward establishing the research university that Gilman had tried to create twenty-five years earlier. Among the distinguished recruits were Alfred Kroeber in anthropology, Herbert Bolton in history, and Joel Hildebrand in chemistry. The careers of these faculty giants

FIGURE 13. Theodore Roosevelt at Charter Day in the Greek Theater, 1911. Roosevelt, seated in the center, is flanked by Benjamin Ide Wheeler on his left and Phoebe Apperson Hearst on his far right. Bancroft Library, University of California, Berkeley.

extended well beyond the Wheeler era: Hildebrand, for example, was still active in research in the 1980s, when he was in his nineties. Wheeler's reputation helped the university attract such distinguished visitors as President Theodore Roosevelt, who spoke in the new Greek Theater in 1903 and again in 1911.

Wheeler loved German literature and culture, and partly for that reason opposed America's entrance into World War I. Once the decision to go to war was made, he loyally supported the war effort and made the campus available for military programs. But the controversy over his political views weakened his prestige. Sensing an opportunity, the faculty pushed hard for restoration of its lost powers. In the midst of growing difficulties, Wheeler announced his retirement in 1919. Phoebe Apperson Hearst died in the same year. The two people most responsible for the university's extraordinary period of growth and development were gone.

The university's enrollment had increased from fewer than two thousand to more than seven thousand during the two decades of the Hearst-Wheeler era, a growth rate roughly equal to that of the city of Berkeley's population during those years. Obviously, then, the expansion of the university was another factor contributing to the urbanization of the community. Not only did campus growth bring new residents, but the university's burgeoning budget and payroll also contributed to the dynamic growth of the city's economy.

The university's most dramatic influence, however, was not on the material development of the city but on the community's identity and image. In the nineteenth century, ambitious scholars regarded the University of California as a provincial backwater. Josiah Royce, a UC graduate and future philosopher, couldn't wait to leave Berkeley and go to Harvard to establish his scholarly career and reputation. But by the end of the Hearst-Wheeler era, talented young Ivy League academics were coming to Berkeley to establish themselves. Already UC was considered one of America's major institutions of higher learning. The transformed university of the early twentieth century, then, put Berkeley on the map, giving the city a national and even international reputation as a seat of scholarship and learning. To its residents, Berkeley may have been a center of industry and commerce, a place of solid working-class families and pleasant suburban homes, as well as a college town. But to the rest of the world, Berkeley was and remains first and foremost the home of the University of California.

CHAPTER FIVE

A SPECIAL PLACE

In 1905 the newly established Berkeley Chamber of Commerce promoted the city with pamphlets and magazine articles emphasizing the theme of "Berkeley the Beautiful." One of the missives asked, "I suppose omnipotent power could make a better place for a city than Berkeley's location, but has it ever done so?" The rhetoric was not limited to self-interested developers and businessmen. In 1911 the city's Socialist Party mayor, J. Stitt Wilson, proclaimed that "any kind of a day in Berkeley seems sweeter than the best day anywhere else."

All this can be dismissed as typical American boosterism, and surely much of it was. But it is also true that in the midst of the explosive civic growth and development of the early twentieth century, there was a strong sense of Berkeley as a special place, a charmed community of great accomplishment and unlimited potential. This belief was reflected in attempts at social and political reform and efforts to create new living spaces and lifestyles. Back in 1873, Governor Newton Booth had proclaimed Berkeley the "Athens of the West," but in the early twentieth century,

FIGURE 14. Berkeley boosters: the cover of a Chamber of Commerce brochure, ca. 1907. Berkeley Historical Society, Berkeley, CA.

some Berkeleyans seemed to be trying to achieve the "Utopia of the Pacific."

Much of this spirit was due to the presence of the University of California. Attracting scholars, intellectuals, and idealistic, enthusiastic young people, the university was laying a social foundation for utopian aspirations. In addition, the university attracted residents who, while not formally affiliated with the institution, still wanted to live in what they believed to be the edifying intellectual and cultural atmosphere of a college town.

A bevy of religious institutions also influenced community life. Beginning with the establishment of Congregationalist and Catholic parishes in the 1870s, Berkeley had by the early 1900s become a proud city of churches. A strong current of Protestant morality affected public policies, from the prohibition of alcoholic beverages to the fight against political corruption. The city was also the location of several church schools, including the California Theological Seminary, which in 1905 moved to Scenic and Le-Conte avenues, just north of the university campus. It changed its name to the Pacific School of Religion in 1916 and became the hub of the affiliated church schools and institutes that formed the Graduate Theological Union in 1962. "Holy Hill," just north of campus, remains an important symbol of the strong moral tone that religious institutions have often contributed to Berkeley public life.

CIVIC CHUTZPAH

The Chamber of Commerce's most ambitious early twentieth-century activity, however, was more a matter of civic chutzpah and pecuniary interest than religious morality. In 1907 the chamber began a campaign to move the state capital to Berkeley. Louis Titus, a partner with Duncan McDuffie in the development of the new Northbrae neighborhood, first suggested the idea. Not surprisingly, Titus recommended that the capitol building be located in Northbrae, at the base of the North Berkeley hills. Two wide boulevards, Marin Avenue and Hopkins Street east of the Alameda, were planned as dramatic access routes to the proposed seat of government. Warming to their task, the developers named most of the streets in the new neighborhood after California counties, and John Galen Howard was commissioned to design elaborate entrance pillars and the landscaped Marin Circle. (A fountain designed by Howard and originally located in the circle was restored in the 1990s.) The legislature agreed to put the issue on the 1908 state ballot, but the voters decisively rejected the move, with only Alameda, San Francisco, and Santa Clara counties supporting the proposal. Still, it is intriguing to speculate what the 1960s in Berkeley would have been like if Governor Ronald Reagan and the state legislature had been located just a mile or so north of the campus protests.

Some of the city's other promotional programs were more successful. For example, in 1914 the Southern Pacific finally agreed to make Berkeley a regular stop on its West Berkeley main line. Eventually, the SP built a terminal at the foot of University Avenue. (During the 1980s and 90s, the building served as a restaurant, and in 2002 the city council considered restoring it to its original purpose to serve the increasing amount of California Amtrak passenger traffic. However, the city finally decided to construct only a simple outdoor plaza to accommodate rail patrons.) Also in 1914, the federal government completed another project dear to the Chamber of Commerce: a graceful new post office on Allston Way. The Berkeley chamber worked hard to defeat still another attempt at annexation by Oakland (while Oakland was vigorously opposing San Francisco's plan for a Bay Area regional government based on New York's borough system).

Among American chambers of commerce, Berkeley's was unusual in at least one respect: for several years, its executive director was Charles Keeler, an established poet, writer, and naturalist. Even the chamber, however, was unable to overcome the economic and sectional differences that divided the Berkeley business community. The Chamber of Commerce members were primarily downtown and East Berkeley merchants, real-estate developers, and professionals. In 1905 West Berkeley industrialists, like their counterparts in many other American cities, formed their own organization, the Berkeley Manufacturers' Association.

WOMEN'S RIGHTS

Compared with the concerns of the chamber of commerce, the fight for women's rights and suffrage was more indicative of the moralistic tone of Berkeley politics during the early twentieth century. As we have seen, church women were active in the campaign to ban alcoholic beverages, and many Berkeleyans got their first experience in community affairs through the good offices of the Women's Christian Temperance Union. Not surprisingly, the WCTU championed the suffrage cause. Though often primarily upper-middle-class social organizations, Berkeley women's clubs also took stands on public issues and frequently supported the suffrage movement and other reforms.

The university had officially been coeducational since 1870, and university women were another important source of support for women's voting rights. The Regents decreed that women should be admitted to UC on "equal terms in all respects with young men." The first woman graduated from Cal in 1876, and the university awarded its first doctoral degree to a woman in 1898. Nevertheless, female students were sometimes harassed by male classmates and greeted with open hostility by some male faculty. Conditions improved markedly during the Hearst-Wheeler era, in part because of the great influence of Phoebe Apperson Hearst herself. In addition to establishing scholarships and facilities for women students, she personally paid for a half-time doctor, Mary Bennet Ritter, to provide health care for university women.

Women benefited from the establishment of the first teaching-certificate program in the 1890s. At that time, about 90 percent of employed female college graduates in the United States worked as teachers, so a teacher-training program naturally attracted women students. By 1906, Cal had about two thousand women on its rolls, more than 90 percent of whom were applying for teacher's certificates, and the education department had the university's largest graduate enrollment. Also in 1906, Benjamin Ide Wheeler appointed Lucy Sprague as the first dean of women. A year later, Jessica Peixotto, an 1894 UC graduate, became the first tenure-track female faculty member (in social economics). Between 1911 and 1916, women made up between 40 and 50 percent of the annual undergraduate admissions at Cal. By the early twentieth century, then, the campus area was home to an extraordinary concentration of well-educated young women, many of whom were likely recruits to the suffragist cause.

One of the important Berkeley suffrage activists was Mary McHenry Keith, a UC graduate who was the first woman to earn a law degree at Hastings College. She was a leader of the Berkeley Political Equality League and one of the organizers of the Woman's Congress that met in Berkeley in 1895. During that meeting, she and her husband, the artist and conservationist William Keith, entertained Susan B. Anthony at their Berkeley home. In 1896 another Berkeley activist, Theresa Jacquemine, refused to leave the Alameda County Recorder's office, chaining herself to a desk until she was allowed to register to vote. The deputy recorder finally let her register, but the district attorney removed her name after she left the premises. That piece of political theater apparently had little effect. In 1896 California (male) voters overwhelmingly defeated a measure to establish female suffrage in the state. Fifteen years later, however, a similar proposal finally passed by a narrow margin, and California became the sixth state in the United States to allow women to vote. While Alameda County as a whole voted solidly against the measure, in Berkeley it passed.

After the establishment of women's suffrage in 1911, suffrage supporters organized the League of Women Voters. The league has been an influential, nonpartisan force in Berkeley politics ever since. Berkeley women's clubs also remained active after the establishment of suffrage. In the late 1920s several previously separate organizations joined together to form the Berkeley Women's City Club. Its building on Durant Avenue, designed by Julia Morgan and completed in 1930, is a Berkeley landmark. In 1923 there

FIGURE 15. Designed by Julia Morgan, the Berkeley
Women's City Club (now Berkeley City Club) opened
in 1930. Berkeley City Club Photo Archive, Berkeley, CA.

were enough women teaching at the university to warrant the construction of a Women's Faculty Club, still another of John Galen
Howard's distinguished campus structures.

REFORM POLITICS

While California was approving women's suffrage in 1911, Berkeley voters were electing the state's first Socialist mayor. The So-

cialist Party was a viable political organization in early twentieth-century America, offering reformist and radical political alternatives to the platforms of the mainstream parties. Although Socialist Party supporters often differed violently among themselves over program and ideology, they did at least agree on measures to reduce poverty, empower working people, and establish government ownership of public utilities and basic industries. The early 1910s were the high point of Socialist Party influence in California, the party's candidate for mayor of Los Angeles coming within a few thousand votes of winning the 1910 election.

J. Stitt Wilson, a Canadian-born Methodist minister, was Berkeley's leading Socialist. He preached a form of the "social gospel," which unified Christianity and socialism into a neat ideological package. (However, neither his political nor his religious convictions prevented him from repeating California's dominant anti-Asian rhetoric.) As the Socialist candidate for governor in 1910, Wilson won a respectable 12 percent of the vote. In the following year, he was the party's unanimous candidate for mayor of Berkeley. He won a narrow victory by combining the votes of some East Berkeley reformers with solid working-class support in West Berkeley. In fact, Wilson won every precinct west of Shattuck Avenue. He campaigned on a "big government" platform of city ownership of public utilities and a substantial program of civic improvements. Unable to get his programs through a hostile city council, Wilson declined to stand for reelection in 1913, choosing instead to run for the congressional seat held by the Republican congressman and future newspaper publisher Joseph Knowland. In that election, Wilson managed to win 40 percent of the vote against a powerful, conservative incumbent.

In spite of Berkeley's brief fling with socialism, for most of the early twentieth century, conventional "progressive" reformers dominated the city's politics. Like progressives in other parts of the country, Berkeley reformers tried to make government more honest, efficient, and responsive to middle-class voters. In 1907 William Carey Jones, dean of the university's School of Jurisprudence, argued that in the old days, Berkeley had been "too small to offer much temptation to the professional politician. There was nothing to be boss of." But rapid growth and urbanization had changed all that, creating the "exploitation of the city for the benefit of the organization, of the machine. . . . This shame," he said, "has already fallen on Berkeley."

To reverse this sad state of affairs, Jones proposed a new city charter which would restore at-large elections of city council members and introduce direct democracy provisions: the initiative, referendum, and recall. Jones also championed the nonpartisan commission form of government, in which each council member served as a commissioner with administrative authority over one or more city departments. In 1909 voters approved the new charter, but soon critics were complaining that council members were more concerned about the interests of their particular departments than the good of the city as a whole. Reformers led by Professor Samuel May, director of the university's Bureau of Public Administration, proposed a city-manager form of government, vesting day-to-day administrative power in a professional manager and limiting elected officials to broad policy-making functions. The proposal won the support of many businessmen, who admired its purported efficiency. Benjamin Ide Wheeler was a strong supporter, arguing that the concept worked well in Germany. Nevertheless, voters defeated the city-manager system in 1916, apparently swayed by arguments that it took too much power away from elected officials. The proposal was adopted in 1923, however, and has operated in Berkeley ever since.

In addition to establishing the city-manager form of government, Berkeley attempted to professionalize and depoliticize most other local-government functions. In the early twentieth century, the city established a civil-service system for public employees and created a professional fire department, ending two decades of volunteer fire stations in the community. But the most extensive program of professionalization, one that set a powerful national example, occurred in the Berkeley Police Department. In 1905 August Vollmer was elected town marshal. A Louisiana native who served in the Spanish-American War, Vollmer used his veteran status to become a Berkeley postman. He was an intelligent, friendly man, and reformers supported his candidacy for marshal as part of an effort to fight corruption and crime, which were perceived to be particular problems in West Berkeley. When the 1909 charter established a professional police department and eliminated the elected office of town marshal, Vollmer was appointed the city's first police chief.

Over the next three decades, Vollmer established what was widely regarded as a model force. He ended graft, introduced scientific methods of investigation, and established educational requirements and professional standards. He literally put the cops on wheels, first establishing bike patrols, then introducing motorcycles in 1912 and cars in 1914. The Berkeley police department developed the first lie detector and was among the earliest to use fingerprints and radios. As part of his crime-prevention effort, Vollmer founded the Junior Police, which eventually evolved into the nation's first junior traffic patrol. Vollmer also hired the nation's first college-trained policewoman, Elizabeth Lossing, and Berkeley's first African American officer, Walter Gordon. A Cal graduate who had been an All-American football player, Officer Gordon patrolled on the night shift while attending Boalt Law School and serving as assistant football coach during the day. In spite of this excruciating schedule, he managed to graduate from Boalt and become a distinguished lawyer and public official, eventually serving as territorial governor of the U.S. Virgin Islands.

Vollmer had only a seventh-grade education, but he was proud that his force had so many college-educated officers like Lossing and Gordon. He started the nation's first college-level criminology department at Cal and worked with a great variety of police departments, including those in Chicago, Los Angeles, and Havana, to establish training methods and professional standards. In Berkeley these standards produced a more honest, more efficient, and less brutal police force than existed in most American cities. But, as with so many progressive reforms, professionalization may have helped alienate public servants from the very public they were supposed to serve. Career police officers and fire fighters, like career city managers and other officials, were sometimes more loyal to their professional community and its standards than to the cities and citizens for whom they worked. At times the reformers' attempts to achieve honest and efficient government seemed to outweigh any commitment to participatory democracy.

Vollmer's faith in education was typical of his generation of reformers. Berkeley was very much affected by the Progressive Education movement of these years. The school district began enforcing school attendance laws, and, as a result, postelementary enrollment substantially increased. Berkeley High School expanded its facilities and curriculum, and, along with a community in Illinois, Berkeley pioneered the development of the junior high school. But within these expanded secondary schools, tracking became the rule, with a high percentage of West Berkeley working-class students, often from immigrant families, relegated to noncollegiate vocational programs. The university played an important role in the California educational system, as UC entrance requirements determined high school college-preparation curricula throughout the state. For many years, university faculty

FIGURE 16. August Vollmer (right) with UC president
Robert Gordon Sproul, 1936. Under Vollmer's leadership, the Berkeley Police Department pioneered in
scientific crime fighting techniques, including the use
of fingerprints. Bancroft Library, University of California, Berkeley.

had the power to accredit the state's high schools, and the UC education department helped promote the establishment of public junior colleges. The department also cooperated with the Berkeley school district in operating an experimental elementary school on the site of what is now the Jewish Community Center on Walnut Street.

BERKELEY BOHEMIA

While Berkeley government and public education were undergoing substantial changes in the early twentieth century, the residents of what some Berkeleyans called "Nut Hill" were engaging in social and cultural experiments, involving new concepts of living spaces and lifestyles. Nut Hill encompassed a somewhat ill-defined hillside area north of campus and east of Euclid Avenue. The name may have referred either to the vegetarian diet of some of the residents or to the fact that some hill-dwellers had lifestyles their fellow citizens considered downright weird. The origins of the neighborhood's special reputation go back to 1894, when Charles Keeler engaged Bernard Maybeck to design a home at the corner of Highland Place and Ridge Road. A poet and naturalist, Keeler had little use for the elaborate Victorian houses that had been popular in the late nineteenth century. He believed they were profoundly unnatural and inappropriate for the kind of community he hoped to promote in the Berkeley Hills. He asked Maybeck for a house that blended into its natural surroundings and projected a simple, healthy lifestyle for its inhabitants.

Maybeck's design, his first in Berkeley, was for an unpainted redwood structure with shingle siding, exposed beams and rafters, steep rooflines, and a handsome stone fireplace. The house was not only consistent with Keeler's ideas but also helped establish a tradition of Bay Area home building that was to last for much

FIGURE 17. Bernard Maybeck, Berkeley's influential architect, master crafts-
man, and bohemian iconoclast photographed at Bohemian Grove, 1932.
Bernard Maybeck Collection (1956-1) Environmental Archives, University
of California, Berkeley.

of the twentieth century. (Joseph Worcester, who built woodsy cottages in Piedmont and San Francisco, introduced the style to the region even before Maybeck's work on the Keeler house.) Many other Berkeley architects, including John Galen Howard and Julia Morgan, followed Maybeck's lead, building houses in what became a particular Bay Area expression of the larger Arts and Crafts Movement. Morgan's design for the original St. John's Presbyterian Church on College Avenue, now the Julia Morgan Center for the Performing Arts, is a fine institutional example of the genre. Like Morgan and Howard, Maybeck designed buildings in many other styles, including the wonderfully gaudy Palace of Fine Arts in San Francisco and the reinforced concrete, "earthquake-proof" house on La Loma Avenue commissioned by the geology professor Andrew Lawson after the 1906 quake. But Maybeck returned again and again to the plain, natural character he had captured in the Keeler house. It characterizes two of his most notable Berkeley buildings: the Faculty Club on campus and the First Church of Christ Scientist on Dwight Way.

In 1898 Keeler's ideas were a major force behind the establishment of the Hillside Club. Its members included the architects John Galen Howard, Almeric Coxhead, and Bernard Maybeck, as well as Maybeck's wife, Annie, who was one of the organization's most influential founders. The club was dedicated to a new kind of urban development that would respect rather than destroy the natural environment. In the North Berkeley hills, club members were determined to retain the natural topography and produce "artistic homes that appear to have grown out of the hillside and to be a part of it." They opposed streets laid out on the grid plan, calling instead for winding lanes that followed the contours of the land. They also advocated a network of pedestrian paths and fought any attempt to cut down the region's trees. A club pamphlet said, "The few native trees that have survived centuries should be jealously preserved. . . . Bend the road, divide the lots, place the houses to accommodate them!" Annie Maybeck was particularly protective of native trees, often taking on City Hall on their behalf. One block of Le Roy Avenue was divided specifically to save what came to be known as "Annie's Oak." In 1904 the club published Keeler's *The Simple Home*, an extended essay outlining his views on architecture and its relation to the good and proper life. The book was dedicated to "My Friend and Counselor Bernard Maybeck."

Maybeck claimed the perfect California home was a well-vegetated hillside with "a few rooms scattered around in case it rains." He loved telling stories about the shocked reaction of neighbors as they saw the Keeler house being built. He became a vegetarian, kept a beard long after it was fashionable, and often wore a beret. When their son was born, he and Annie believed that giving him a name would stunt the development of the child's individuality. They called him "Boy" for the first few years of his life, until he was old enough to choose his own name. My great-grandfather, Louis Wollenberg, lived around the corner from the Maybecks at the time. After spending more than forty years failing at a number of business ventures in the American West, Louis had retired, living off his several children. He spent his time telling stories (some of which may even have been true) about his adventures to the neighborhood kids. When asked what name he wanted, "Boy" Maybeck said, "Wollenberg." This was a bit too much even for his bohemian parents, so they compromised and agreed to call him "Wallen." But even with this concession to normalcy, Bernard and Annie Maybeck were what most early twentieth-century Americans would have considered unconventional.

Even more unconventional were Florence and Treadwell Boynton. In 1911 they bought a lot from Maybeck on Buena Vista Way and had him draw up plans for the most unusual of all the homes

FIGURE 18. The Boynton family's Temple of Wings, built on "Nut Hill" in 1914. Dimitri Shipounoff Collection, Berkeley Architectural Heritage Association, Berkeley, CA.

on Nut Hill. The Boyntons and Maybecks soon began what turned out to be a two-decade feud, so the structure was completed under the direction of a different architect. In 1914 the Boyntons moved into the Temple of Wings, a hillside platform with a roof supported by thirty-four Corinthian columns. Until 1923, the structure had no walls, though sailcloth could be deployed in case of heavy wind and rain. The Boyntons often wore togas and robes and lived mostly on fruits and nuts. Florence Boynton was a friend and follower of the modern dancer Isadora Duncan, and the temple was sometimes a venue for Duncan's performances. The tradition was passed on to the Boyntons' daughter, Sulgwynn, who, along with her husband Charles Quitzow, gave modern dance lessons to several generations of young Berkeleyans. As late as the

1980s, when the Quitzows were themselves in their eighties, Sulgwynn was still teaching dance to young girls in robes amid the gardens and columns of the Temple of Wings.

"PROGRESSIVE" DEVELOPMENT

As unconventional as some of the residents of Nut Hill may have been, the Hillside Club also included such establishment figures as John Galen Howard and the real-estate developer Frank Wilson. Even though he was not a member, Duncan McDuffie, one of Berkeley's most active early developers, was also in sympathy with many of the club's principles. In 1905 McDuffie established a partnership with David Mason, who had opened a real-estate office on Shattuck Avenue in the mid-1880s. As Mason was approaching retirement, McDuffie became the leading partner, and he involved the firm in joint ventures with some of the biggest East Bay developers, including Borax Smith, Frank Havens, and John Spring. McDuffie also considered himself a committed conservationist, and in this respect he was carrying on an important Berkeley tradition: Jeanne Carr, the wife of Cal's first professor of agriculture, along with William Keith, Joseph and John LeConte, and other prominent Berkeley residents, had helped John Muir establish the Sierra Club in 1892. McDuffie was also a prominent member of the Sierra Club and served as president of the Save the Redwoods League. In addition, he was an early and influential advocate for the California state-park system.

Like many progressive realtors of his day, McDuffie expressed his conservation consciousness through support of developments that featured lush landscaping, curving and irregular street patterns, and substantial open space. These "cities in a garden" were immensely popular and thus appealed to the developers' profit motives as well as their aesthetic sensibilities. Two of the most dra-

matic examples in the Bay Area were Mason-McDuffie's Claremont district in Berkeley and St. Francis Wood in San Francisco.
These were high-end projects, appealing to wealthy home buyers, but McDuffie built similar, if less elaborate, amenities into new
middle-income neighborhoods like Northbrae. Even San Pablo
Park, a working-class development in southwest Berkeley, was
built around a large public park that was donated to the city.

McDuffie was a strong proponent of city zoning. In 1916
Berkeley became the second community in California (after Los
Angeles) and one of the earliest in the nation to establish a city
planning commission. Over the next few years, various parts of the
city were zoned residential, commercial, and so on. The zoning
protected many of the bucolic new neighborhoods from overde-
velopment, but it also promoted the separation of home and work.
Ocean View, or West Berkeley, had originally developed as a place
where people both lived and worked, but as much of the area was
zoned industrial, homes declined in value and were destroyed to
make way for new manufacturing plants. Not until the 1970s were
effective steps taken to preserve some of the oldest residential
buildings and blocks in the city, and by then much of the original Ocean View had been lost.

In Berkeley, as in many other American cities, restrictive zoning was often accompanied by restrictive covenants. These were
provisions attached to deeds by which developers prohibited buyers from subsequently selling or renting their property to "undesirable" individuals, which in Berkeley meant Asians and African
Americans. In addition to the covenants, which had become common in Berkeley neighborhoods by the 1920s, real-estate brokers
tried to prevent people of color from buying or renting in other
"white" areas of the city. The result was that almost all Asian and
black Berkeleyans lived south of Dwight Way and west of Grove
Street. When George Shima, a prominent Japanese immigrant

who had become a wealthy agriculturalist, built a house on College Avenue, he faced so much harassment from white neighbors that he had to erect a large fence around his lot. And when Dwight Uchida, an executive of a Japanese trading company, rented a home on Stuart Street, he was visited by a delegation of neighbors asking him to move. The house was a few yards east of Grove and thus barely on the wrong side of an invisible but very real dividing line. Berkeley may have been a special place in the early twentieth century, but not so special as to escape the devastating effects of traditional American racism.

CHAPTER SIX

BOOM AND BUST

The emblems of the "Roaring Twenties"—bathtub gin, the Charleston, flappers—were manifestations of a great consumer-oriented economic boom. During the twenties the United States became the world's first mass-consumption industrial society, and the result was a decade of material prosperity and growth that benefited many, though by no means all, of its residents. California was the boom state of that boom decade, the population increasing by about 60 percent in just ten years. Berkeley also boomed, its population growing from 56,000 to 82,000, a rate of increase almost matching that of the state as a whole. But after the stock market crash of 1929, the boom turned to bust for the nation, the state, and Berkeley. Precisely because this mass-consumption economy encompassed so much of the population, the Great Depression had a broader public impact than any previous economic downturn. In the midst of that two-decade cycle of boom and bust, the Berkeley that we know today began to emerge. Physically, at least, the Berkeley of 1940 looked very much like the Berkeley of 2000.

FIRE IN BERKELEY

Although the 1920s were a period of tremendous material growth, the most dramatic event of the decade in Berkeley was a great natural disaster. In the early afternoon of September 17, 1923, a fire began in Wildcat Canyon, in what is today Tilden Park. It was a hot fall day, and, fueled by a strong, dry northeasterly wind, the fire crested the hills and raced down the canyon of Codornices Creek into populated parts of North Berkeley. The fire proceeded in an irregular southwesterly direction, reaching as far as Hearst Avenue on the south and, in a few places, Shattuck Avenue on the west. The blaze was more than a match for the Berkeley Fire Department, so Chief G. Sydney Rose called in help from Oakland, Richmond, Emeryville, Piedmont, and San Francisco. The San Francisco units, arriving by ferry about ninety minutes after they were called, stationed themselves at University and Shattuck avenues and were credited with saving the downtown. Hundreds of university students were massed along Hearst and kept the flames from crossing into the campus. But the fire continued burning until the wind shifted to the southwest, when the cool ocean breeze blew the flames back on themselves and allowed firefighters to extinguish the blaze.

The conflagration resulted in no deaths or serious injuries, but it destroyed 584 buildings and seriously damaged more than 30 others. The total economic loss was about ten million dollars, and approximately four thousand people were left homeless. The city government and Red Cross struggled to find temporary quarters for the homeless, and, in a reversal of the 1906 experience, many refugees found immediate shelter in San Francisco. Four days after the fire, the city planning commission met to organize the rapid reconstruction of the area. Displaced residents and community groups demanded a considerable role in the process, Bernard May-

FIGURE 19. Aerial view of the destruction caused by the 1923 fire (note the devastated neighborhoods north of campus). Bancroft Library, University of California, Berkeley.

beck even proposing that neighborhood blocks do their own planning. This was a bit too much for the commission, but, in the end, the city agreed to residents' wishes to maintain the north campus district primarily as a residential neighborhood of single-family homes. However, the business block on Euclid Avenue was rebuilt, and in the area immediately adjacent to the campus substantial numbers of apartment houses rose from the ashes.

After seeing the flames quickly spread from roof to roof, Bernard Maybeck vowed never to build another wood-shingle house. The city council followed suit, unanimously voting to outlaw shingle roofs. But lumber-industry trade associations, fearing a precedent that might spread to other communities, vehemently objected to the ordinance and in 1924 sponsored an initiative that repealed the council action. Maybeck's partner, John White, agreed to design a shingle replacement for the burned Hillside Clubhouse, but most property owners had learned a painful lesson. Influenced by the popularity of the Mission Revival and Mediterranean architectural styles, they rebuilt with stucco siding and tiled roofs. Not until the 1970s did wood-shingle houses come back into style in Berkeley.

Today, the fire's erratic course can still be easily traced by walking north from the UC campus on streets like Arch or Spruce. Older wood-sided buildings that escaped the path of the blaze interrupt the blocks of stucco homes built after 1923. For several years, the city operated a fire lookout station on Grizzly Peak during the summer. But most of the lessons of 1923 were gradually forgotten, and the even more destructive 1991 East Bay hills fire found the community almost as unprepared as it had been in the early twenties. While most of the damage was in Oakland, the 1991 blaze destroyed several southeastern Berkeley hillside homes. One important lesson that had to be relearned in 1991 was the need for effective communication between the Berkeley and Oakland fire departments, as well as between those departments and the autonomous firefighting units of the East Bay Regional Park District and the Lawrence Berkeley Laboratory.

In 1923, as city officials had hoped, reconstruction was rapid. The number of building permits issued by the city grew from a healthy 2,182 in 1922 to an extraordinary 4,293 in 1925. By no means did all of this construction occur in the burned area. Acres of new homes went up on the northern and southern edges of the city. By the 1930s, Berkeley was essentially built out, with undeveloped open space mainly limited to a large university-owned tract in northwest Berkeley and Park Hills, adjacent to Tilden Park.

These areas were developed after World War II, the city annexing Park Hills in 1958 in Berkeley's last territorial expansion.

There was plenty of commercial construction as well, particularly in the downtown area and along Telegraph Avenue. Included was the 1925 American Trust Building, the city's first skyscraper (now the Wells Fargo Building). The boom also affected West Berkeley's manufacturing sector. The number of plants grew from 113 in 1919 to 193 in 1928, and the total annual value of goods manufactured in the city increased from $28,000,000 to more than $60,000,000 during those years. Substantial growth also occurred in North Oakland and Albany, so that, by the early thirties, Berkeley was part of a continuous urban corridor extending from East Oakland to El Cerrito.

REGIONAL WATER AND PARK SYSTEMS

The 1923 fire revealed some serious deficiencies in Berkeley's water system. When homeowners turned on their hoses at the same time that firefighters connected hoses to their hydrants, water pressure dropped to near zero. Complaints about water service had been expressed for decades. After Henry Berryman sold his original Berkeley waterworks in the 1880s, the city had been integrated into a series of privately owned regional systems that included Oakland. The most ambitious of these, the People's Water Company, controlled by the former Smith-Havens syndicate, went bankrupt in 1914 in the midst of a serious drought. New investors hastily organized the East Bay Water Company and took measures to increase supply, including building the San Pablo Reservoir and developing the Wildcat Creek watershed, but these were short-term solutions at best. By 1920 several firms, including the Goodyear Tire Company, had decided not to locate in the East Bay because of the inadequate water service.

East Bay business and political leaders concluded that if the region was to continue its rapid economic and population growth, it had to follow the examples of Los Angeles and San Francisco and develop a publicly owned system that tapped the apparently inexhaustible watersheds of the Sierra Nevada. Some Berkeley politicians favored buying into San Francisco's Hetch Hetchy system, but Oakland leaders viewed this option as another plot to bring the region under San Francisco control. Instead, East Bay movers and shakers finally agreed to a plan long advocated by the former Oakland mayor and California governor George Pardee. Pardee argued for a separate water district that would build a Sierra system for the urbanized parts of the East Bay, including Oakland, Alameda, Richmond, and Berkeley. The state legislature authorized the establishment of the East Bay Municipal Utility District in 1921, and two years later the new EBMUD board chose the Mokelumne River in the central Sierra Nevada as the source of supply. In 1924 voters approved a bond issue to pay for the project by a three-to-one margin. Five years later, Mokelumne River water from Pardee Reservoir, about one hundred miles east of Berkeley, flowed out of East Bay taps for the first time.

The new district purchased the assets of the old East Bay Water Company but had no use for the Wildcat Creek watershed. Conservationists, led by the Berkeley resident Robert Sibley, director of the UC Alumni Association, revived a plan, first proposed in the 1860s by Frederick Law Olmsted, to preserve the East Bay hills as parkland. But EBMUD, led by George Pardee, refused to participate and prepared to sell Wildcat Canyon to private developers. As a result, open-space supporters, including prominent business and labor leaders, organized the East Bay Park Association and successfully lobbied the legislature to establish still another regional district, this time for park purposes.

The East Bay Regional Park District, the first such agency in the United States, was created in 1933. In the following year, in spite of the deep national depression, East Bay voters agreed to tax themselves to operate the new district and purchase the former watershed land. Two-thousand-acre Tilden Park, named after the park district's first president, was the beginning of what today is a hundred-thousand-acre regional park system in Alameda and Contra Costa counties. Park district land, combined with the adjoining EBMUD watershed, gives the East Bay a remarkable urban greenbelt that is one of its most important public amenities. But the two regional authorities, EBMUD and EBRPD, are powerful government agencies whose elected boards operate with little media attention and almost no public scrutiny.

ROARING TWENTIES UNIVERSITY

As the city and region developed their infrastructure and amenities, the university continued its physical and institutional growth. The student population increased from about seven thousand to more than eleven thousand during the 1920s, and John Galen Howard's building program continued, even after he resigned as university architect in 1923. Within the university hierarchy, much of the 1920s was consumed by the faculty's struggle to reassert its power after the autocratic Wheeler era. But while the faculty fought for more authority over academic and budget matters, it was more than willing to give up most of its control over students' nonacademic life. Freed from old constraints, many students entered into the liberated lifestyle of the twenties with a vengeance. Fraternities and sororities prospered, and although their members did not constitute a majority of the student body, they often controlled student life and politics. If the twenties actually roared anywhere in Berkeley, it was probably among free-spirited and socially active UC students.

The university was most visible to the general public through its athletic programs. Intramural athletics began on an informal basis in the 1870s and grew in importance after completion of the original Harmon Gym in 1879. Intercollegiate sports developed in the 1880s, and in 1895 the track team traveled east and defeated what were considered some of the best squads in the country. These victories produced an outpouring of school spirit: the English professor Charles Mills Gayley was even moved to write a university song. During the 1899 championship baseball game with Stanford, Cal students stole a Stanford axe, and that trophy eventually became the prize awarded to the winner of the annual Big Game football extravaganza. Benjamin Ide Wheeler outlawed football for a few years, but the sport made a spectacular comeback in the 1920s. Under coach Andy Smith, the "Wonder Teams" were undefeated in fifty straight games between 1920 and 1925, outscoring their opponents 1,649 to 139. The winning streak included five consecutive victories over the hated rival Stanford and two Rose Bowl appearances.

At Cal, as at other major universities, football became big business, an important part of the mass-consumption society of the 1920s. The games attracted tens of thousands of people who had no connection with the school other than identification with the team. Athletic success brought the university public recognition and opened the hearts and checkbooks of wealthy alumni and other potential donors. Not surprisingly, Cal fans lobbied for a football stadium that would reflect the new public significance of the sport.

In 1921 a major subscription drive raised more than a million dollars to build the new stadium. It was to be dedicated to the memory of university graduates who died in World War I, giving the project a patriotic as well as athletic cachet. For stadium supporters, the preferred site was the mouth of Strawberry

Canyon, one of the loveliest areas on campus and a favorite picnic spot for both students and Berkeley residents. Although many
Berkeleyans protested the destruction of the canyon and John
Galen Howard suggested another location, the proposal had
tremendous popular support and momentum. In a crushing defeat for conservationists, the project went ahead, with builders
excavating the canyon mouth to accommodate the new structure
(which turned out to virtually straddle the Hayward Fault). All
seventy-six thousand seats were filled at Memorial Stadium's
opening, which coincided with the 1923 Big Game (which, of
course, Cal won).

ENTER THE AUTO

The 1920s development that most affected the daily lives of
Berkeley residents was perhaps the emergence of the automobile
as the main means of transportation. Crude horseless carriages had
been around since the end of the nineteenth century, and by 1915
cars were commonly sharing Berkeley's streets with horse-drawn
vehicles and electric trolleys. In the twenties, assembly-line production methods transformed cars into consumer items affordable even for working-class families, and California led the nation and the world into the automobile age. By 1930 there were
more motor vehicles than households in California, one car or
truck for every three residents. In that year, the state had less than
5 percent of the nation's population but nearly 10 percent of the
nation's autos.

Berkeley fully participated in the automobilization of California life. Virtually every home built after World War I had a
garage. The North Campus apartments constructed after the 1923
fire were required to have at least one garage space for every unit.
Before World War I, residential neighborhoods had corner stores

and shopping areas within easy walking distance of every house. But homes built in the upper Berkeley hills during the twenties were a steep mile or more away from the nearest shops: it was assumed that residents would now drive to distant shopping areas. Elementary schools, however, were still built within walking distance of homes; after all, little kids couldn't drive.

Today, politically and environmentally correct Berkeley residents are at least theoretically in favor of mass transit and opposed to smog-belching autos. But in the early twentieth century, cars seemed to be a technology that liberated individuals from the control of great corporate transportation empires like the Southern Pacific and the Key System. Automobiles gave Berkeley residents mobility and freed them from the transit corporations' routes and schedules. But this freedom came at a cost, because the car was supported by a massive public road- and street-building program. In 1923 the state legislature passed the gasoline tax, a levy on each gallon of gas sold. A portion of the receipts went for state highways, but part of the tax was returned to local governments for use on streets and roads. Thus Berkeley gained revenue to pave most of its streets and lay out new ones. Unlike almost any other state program, the gas tax gave streets and highways a built-in source of revenue that didn't need specific legislative appropriations each year. California had decided to devote the great bulk of its public transportation dollars to the automobile.

While public tax dollars built streets and roads, private transit companies like the Key System still had to build and maintain their own tracks and pay franchise fees and property taxes to cities and counties. The growing numbers of autos on the road produced traffic jams that caused transit delays, throwing off schedules and making rail commutes less dependable. During the boom years of the twenties, there was plenty of business for both autos and rail transit. But in the thirties, population growth slowed drastically and the bottom fell out of the economy. Private rail systems found it increasingly difficult to compete against the publicly subsidized automobile. Key System patronage declined and the company, whose finances had never been strong, began to sustain heavy losses.

San Francisco Bay had prevented the final victory of the automobile during the twenties. Even before World War I, the region's traditional transportation system attempted to adjust to the new reality by establishing automobile ferries between Oakland and San Francisco. In 1926 the Golden Gate Ferry Company, a Southern Pacific affiliate, inaugurated service on a Berkeley–San Francisco line, operating from a new Berkeley pier that extended out to deep water three miles into the bay. The new ferry was Berkeley's first direct transit connection with San Francisco in nearly fifty years. Although the company provided bus service along University Avenue for patrons without cars, the 1926 system was primarily an auto ferry. As such, it was obsolete even before it was completed. Big Game days created the greatest traffic jams in Berkeley history, with cars backed up the length of the pier and on to University Avenue waiting to board the ferry. What the new automobile age demanded was a bridge across the bay.

In 1929 the federal government allocated funds to build the Oakland–San Francisco Bay Bridge. Just two years after completion of the project in 1936, Golden Gate Ferry called it quits. The company gave its Berkeley pier to the city, and a small portion of it still serves as a public fishing and recreation facility. Originally, the lower deck of the Bay Bridge was designed to accommodate electric trains. But in 1941 both the Southern Pacific and Sacramento Northern ended electric passenger service, leaving the Key System as the surviving rail transit provider. The company enjoyed some success during World War II because of gas rationing

FIGURE 20. Sign at the corner of San Pablo and University Avenues, marking the way to the Berkeley ferry pier, ca. 1930. Berkeley Historical Society, Berkeley, CA.

and population growth, but after the war patronage fell like a rock, declining 42 percent between 1949 and 1952 alone.

The system was acquired by National City Lines, a holding company owned by Firestone Tires, Phillips Petroleum, Standard Oil of California, Mack Trucks, and General Motors, among others. Given the nature of its ownership, it is hardly a surprise that National City favored gas-powered, internal combustion vehicles that ran on rubber tires. The new management phased out inner-city trolleys, replacing the rail cars with buses. Rail service continued only on the transbay routes across the bridge. But the system kept on losing money and in 1958 was merged into the new Alameda–Contra Costa Transit District, a public agency supported by local taxes. AC Transit ended the last transbay rail service, replacing the trains with buses and allowing the bridge to be retrofitted with two one-way decks. Ironically, this change occurred just as planning began for a Bay Area Rapid Transit Dis-

FIGURE 21. Key System F Train to San Francisco, Shattuck Avenue, ca. 1940. Bancroft Library, University of California, Berkeley.

trict, destined to replicate much of the old Key route with a new rail system.

NEW DEAL PROJECTS

Although the federal government allocated the funds for the Bay Bridge during the administration of Herbert Hoover, construction took place in the Roosevelt years. The project was among the many public-works projects that Franklin Roosevelt's New Deal built to promote economic recovery from the Depression. Included was the first bore of the Lower Broadway (now Caldecott) Tunnel, also constructed in the thirties with federal funds. It created the first convenient automobile link between Berkeley (and Oakland) and central Contra Costa County. The bridge and tunnel represented the final triumph of the automobile: now every major East Bay commute route had an easy highway connection.

If the car came of age during the boom years of the twenties, it took the bust of the thirties to produce the huge public-works projects that secured the auto's final victory.

In addition to public-works contracts with private firms, the New Deal also created government job programs to put the unemployed to work. The National Youth Administration provided work-study positions that allowed students at Cal and Berkeley High to remain in school. The Civilian Conservation Corps employed young Berkeley men in conservation and recreation projects. One of the first CCC camps in California was located in Wildcat Canyon, near the current site of the Tilden Park Environmental Education Center. CCC workers built some of the park's most important facilities, including the dam on Lake Anza, the golf course, and many of the picnic grounds. "CCC boys" dug fire trails and hiking paths and planted groves of redwoods and Monterey pines in the East Bay hills.

The biggest of all the New Deal job programs was the Works Progress Administration. In Berkeley, the WPA built the Rose Garden on Euclid Avenue and Aquatic Park near the waterfront and started construction of the yacht harbor at the Berkeley Marina. WPA workers dismantled part of the Brazilian exhibit at the 1939–40 World's Fair on Treasure Island in the bay and relocated it in Tilden Park, where it became the Brazilian Room. They also worked on additions to Berkeley High, including the Community Theater (which was not finished until after World War II). The WPA's Federal Writers' Project hired Berkeley writers and students to produce a number of books, including a history of the city. The WPA theater project in Oakland provided jobs for East Bay actors and production personnel, and art programs hired painters and photographers. These New Deal programs dramatically changed the relationship between the federal government and local communities such as Berkeley. Cer-

FIGURE 22. Berkeley Rose Garden, a WPA project under construction in the 1930s. Berkeley Historical Society, Berkeley, CA.

tainly federal actions like railroad subsidies and college land grants had affected the general development of the city, but the feds had had little direct impact on everyday life during the first eighty years of Berkeley's existence. It is impossible, however, to discuss the city's history after the New Deal without considering the direct effect of federal programs on the lives and times of Berkeley residents.

DEPRESSION UNIVERSITY

The presence of the university shielded Berkeley from the full impact of the Depression. Although the state legislature cut the UC budget in the early thirties, even a somewhat reduced university payroll was an economic lifebelt for the city. Cal's relative prosperity during the Depression was due in part to the political skill of President Robert Gordon Sproul, who took office in 1930. A 1913 UC graduate, Sproul had worked his way up through the university bureaucracy. He was sociable and garrulous (with a speaking voice like a foghorn), and over the years he had established friendships with key faculty members. These served him well, as he calmed much of the conflict that had plagued faculty-administration relations during the 1920s. An important figure in the state Republican Party, Sproul had served as the university's advocate in Sacramento and had ties with legislative leaders. After 1937, he was even able to win small funding increases.

One of Sproul's most serious challenges was a proposal by southern California legislators to establish the Los Angeles campus of the university as a separate state university, with its own board and budget. Berkeley faculty, students, and alumni tended to regard UCLA as an inferior "southern branch," an attitude that angered influential business and political leaders in Los Angeles, by 1930 the state's largest city. To counter the possibility of secession, Sproul argued that the Los Angeles institution was a separate but equal university campus. To make his point, he took up residence in the south for a time, running the statewide university from UCLA. Without quite planning it, and much to the dismay of many Berkeley loyalists, Sproul established the concept of a multicampus UC system. He maintained a single state university but in the process diminished Berkeley's self-proclaimed role as the center of California's higher-education universe.

DEPRESSION ACTIVISM

Sproul also had to deal with activist students. Most UC students remained politically moderate or conservative during the thirties, and the greatest student disorders in Berkeley were drunken riots celebrating the football victories of the 1937 "Thunder Team." Nevertheless, a significant and vocal minority of the student body responded to the Depression with a commitment to radical or reformist political action. Some joined the Young People's Socialist League or the Young Communist League and championed workers' rights and alternatives to capitalism. Others aligned themselves with the less ideological National Student League or the Social Problems Club. The latter sponsored annual "Student Strikes for Peace," large antiwar and anti-ROTC rallies at Sather Gate. Even the official student government, the Associated Students of the University of California, attempted to force local employers to maintain "Fair Bear" standards, including a minimum wage for student employees. The ASUC urged students to patronize only businesses displaying a Fair Bear window sticker indicating compliance.

Some faculty members also became involved in political activism. The physics professor J. Robert Oppenheimer was one of several young faculty who supported leftist causes and discussed Marxist philosophy. The economics professor Paul Taylor and his wife, the photographer Dorothea Lange, documented the terrible conditions of farm labor in California fields and advocated substantial reforms. Powerful agribusiness interests, some closely identified with the university's agricultural sciences and economics programs, pressured Sproul to rein Taylor in, but the professor reported that his academic freedom was never compromised. Sproul, however, did support a ban on communist speakers and faculty and instituted rules that sharply restricted the campus activities of student groups like the Social Problems Club.

One place where activist groups could always gather was Stiles Hall, the off-campus headquarters of the University YMCA. Its director, Harry Kingman, maintained a free-speech, open-forum policy, allowing a wide spectrum of speakers and organizations to use the facility. Kingman was instrumental in establishing the University Students Cooperative Association in 1933. The organization has provided relatively inexpensive co-op student housing at several facilities ever since. The International House, a dormitory accommodating both foreign and domestic students, which opened in 1930, was another institution that generally maintained a free-speech policy in its community programs.

Cooperative enterprises were considered self-help alternatives to private capitalism during the Depression, and Berkeley spawned several new co-op institutions. In 1937 Finnish American residents in West Berkeley opened a cooperative gas station on San Pablo Avenue. At about the same time, a group of East Bay residents, many with university connections, formed a cooperative food-buying club that soon evolved into a small grocery store. In 1940 the two organizations relocated their enterprises to a single shared lot on University Avenue and Acton Street. Seven years later, they merged to form the Consumer Cooperative of Berkeley. Over the next quarter century, the Berkeley Co-op opened several additional retail outlets and a credit union. It grew into the city's largest commercial enterprise and emerged as a powerful community institution. Its bankruptcy and disintegration in 1988 ended the history of what had been the city's largest institutional product of 1930s activism. Today, only the credit union survives.

The university's relative economic strength could not protect West Berkeley industries from the Depression, and working-class unemployment increased sharply. But the economic conditions also promoted new worker militancy and increased union organizing. New Deal legislation protected the collective-bargaining rights of industrial workers for the first time in American history. As a result, unions achieved substantial increases in membership and power during the thirties. In the Bay Area, the key event was the union victory in the 1934 maritime workers' strike, a conflict that included a successful general strike in San Francisco. In the aftermath of this impressive display of economic power, unions began organizing drives around the Bay Area, including successful campaigns at some of Berkeley's largest industrial employers, like Colgate Palmolive, Durkee Foods, and Cutter Laboratories. The Bayer corporation's large Berkeley facility, the successor to Cutter Labs, remains the city's largest unionized private-sector employer.

All of this leftist activism did not, however, represent Berkeley's political mainstream. While California as a whole voted for Franklin D. Roosevelt in 1932, Berkeley turned out solidly for Herbert Hoover. In 1934 Berkeley voters favored the incumbent Republican governor Frank Merriam over his Democratic opponent, the leftist author Upton Sinclair. Activist students may have demonstrated in favor of the maritime workers in 1934, but members of the Cal football team volunteered as strikebreakers. Many Berkeley political and business leaders were shocked at the level of union activism, fearing that the very structure of American economic and political life was at risk. The new social environment of the thirties, then, produced far more controversy than consensus in Berkeley.

Civil rights was an especially controversial issue. Equal treatment for nonwhites was part of the ASUC Fair Bear standards. The campus newspaper, the *Daily Californian*, proposed that landlords who discriminated on the basis of race be removed from the university's "approved housing" list. Faced with substantial opposition from property owners, the UC administration refused to act. But the ASUC itself had problems. Its barbershop in the Stevens Union refused to cut black students' hair. The relatively liberal policies of the International House, located at the top of Bancroft Way, became a particular source of controversy. The building housed foreign and domestic students of all races and nationalities, and its director, Allen Blaisdell, reported that some residents of nearby fraternities argued they should not have to share the neighborhood with "niggers and chinks." The "I-House" also accommodated both male and female students, and some Berkeleyans feared that this policy would promote interracial marriage. Blaisdell told of a conversation at the Women's Faculty Club in which his wife was asked, "Would you want your daughter to marry a Negro?"

The author Yoshiko Uchida grew up in a Japanese immigrant household on Stuart Street during the boom-and-bust period of the 1920s and 30s. In spite of many discriminatory aspects of Berkeley life, she observes that most of her early childhood friends and playmates were white neighbors, sometimes the children of European immigrants. But as she grew older and dating became an issue, social separation increased, and by the time she graduated from Berkeley High, the majority of her close confidants were Japanese Americans. Uchida graduated early and attended Cal. Although she did well in her classes, she and most of her friends worried that racial discrimination would always prevent them from getting jobs appropriate to their level of educational achievement. She also worried about growing international tension between the

United States and Japan. Those fears became a reality on December 7, 1941, when Japan attacked Pearl Harbor. Still, Uchida was so focused on school that after hearing the news on that Sunday morning, she went off to the library to study. Returning home, she learned that federal officers had arrested her father. Her world, and indeed much of the world of prewar Berkeley, was about to be turned upside down.

CHAPTER SEVEN

WORLD WAR II WATERSHED

During the 1940s, the *San Francisco Chronicle* called World War II a "second Gold Rush." The newspaper was referring not to the international combat but to the social, demographic, and economic impact of the war on the San Francisco Bay Area. The war was to the 1940s, 50s, and 60s what the Gold Rush had been to the 1840s, 50s, and 60s: a watershed event that transformed and redefined regional history. In the very broadest sense, the war began what might be called the Bay Area's defense period, a fifty-year span in which defense dollars, policy, and politics, the economic and technological spin-offs from them and the cultural and social protests against them, were the most important factors in regional history. Only the end of the cold war in the early 1990s, followed by the rapid dismantling of virtually all the region's remaining military installations, brought this era to a close. Not only was Berkeley deeply affected by the war and the postwar period, but it also helped create the nuclear specter that was so much a part of the life and culture of those years.

EXODUS

The war produced what, at least until now, was the last major population increase in the city's history. After experiencing virtually no growth in the 1930s, Berkeley's population grew by nearly 40 percent during the 1940s, from about 85,000 to 115,000. In the immediate aftermath of the attack on Pearl Harbor, however, thousands of people left the city, particularly young men and women departing to join the armed forces. And an additional 1,400 or so people of Japanese descent, including Yoshiko Uchida and her family, left involuntarily to take up residence in government internment camps.

President Roosevelt's Executive Order 9066, issued in February 1942, authorized the military to relocate and intern all people of Japanese descent living in California, Oregon, Washington, and part of Arizona. The sole criterion for internment was ethnicity, not nationality, the order applying equally to Japanese-born immigrants and California-born American citizens of Japanese descent. At the end of April 1942, the Uchidas and other Berkeley internees were relocated to Tanforan Race Track in San Mateo County, where they were assigned "apartments" that had once been horse stalls. After about three months at Tanforan, most of the Berkeley internees were transported to a camp at Topaz, Utah, where many remained until the end of the war.

There is no evidence that the internment served any legitimate defense or security purpose. The government did not institute a similar relocation policy for Italian or German Americans, though a relatively small number of Italian and German immigrants were interned, often unjustly. In Hawaii, where people of Japanese descent made up a far larger portion of the population than in California, there was no mass internment. In 1988 Congress provided for a reparations payment of twenty thousand dollars to each surviving internee in partial compensation for the injustice suffered.

While fear and hysteria following the Pearl Harbor attack were partially responsible for the decision to impose the internment, long-standing anti-Asian discrimination also played a major part. As we have seen, Berkeley was by no means immune to these prejudices. Indeed, as late as mid-1941, some residents of the district immediately north of the UC campus were campaigning for restrictive covenants for their area because Japanese American students were moving into the neighborhood.

Even so, no community in California had stronger organized opposition to the internment policy than Berkeley. Most Japanese American families lived in the ethnically mixed South Berkeley neighborhood, and some had developed friendships with their white and black neighbors. At the university, Japanese American students had developed ties with sympathetic professors and students of other ethnic groups. Several faculty members of the Pacific School of Religion had served as ministers and educators in Japan and had come to appreciate the Japanese people and culture. As a result, a small group of Berkeleyans formed the Fair Play Committee to protest the internment. Its members included Harry Kingman of Stiles Hall, Paul Taylor of the economics department, the photographer Dorothea Lange, and Galen Fisher of the Pacific School of Religion. Their protests hardly represented majority opinion in Berkeley, let alone the rest of the state, and they were unable to prevent the relocation. But the committee did maintain contacts with internees and monitor conditions at the camps. At the suggestion of Kingman and Allen Blaisdell, the director of the International House, UC President Sproul called on the government to allow Japanese American students to finish their college education. Because of these efforts, young people like Yoshiko Uchida were able to leave the camps and complete their degrees at colleges and universities in the East and Midwest, outside the West Coast restricted area.

Another gesture of support was a much-debated decision by the First Congregational Church on Channing Way to make its social hall available as the point of embarkation for Berkeley internees. In stark contrast to the hostile send-off that Japanese Americans suffered in most California communities, church members served coffee and cake and even provided toys for the children. The Northern California Branch of the American Civil Liberties Union, which included many active Berkeley members, defied a decision of the national ACLU and took the case of Fred Koramatsu, an East Bay resident who unsuccessfully challenged the internment, all the way to the U.S. Supreme Court. After the war, most Berkeley Japanese American families returned to the city, picking up their lives and careers. But for some, like Yoshiko Uchida's father, it was too late to start again. A confident executive, community leader, and patriarch before the war, Dwight Uchida never recovered fully from the trauma of internment. He was spiritually troubled and physically ill for much of the rest of his life.

MILITARY ESTABLISHMENT

While Japanese Americans were coping with internment, Berkeley was filling up with new residents. Some were armed-forces personnel stationed at the various military installations around San Francisco Bay. In Berkeley the army established Camp Ashby, headquarters for a segregated unit of African American military policemen, near the west end of Ashby Avenue. The navy built the Savo Island housing project for married personnel in South Berkeley. Both services established officers' training programs at UC. The army took over the Bowles Hall dormitory and kept its

FIGURE 23. Antidraft rally, Sather Gate, 1940. Bancroft Library, University of California, Berkeley.

personnel largely separate from the rest of the students. The navy, on the other hand, generally integrated its trainees into the general student body, allowing them to play on university athletic teams and even participate in student government. The navy program took over the International House and several fraternities to house its trainees. By 1944, more than one thousand navy personnel were studying at Cal.

The government built several barrack-like buildings north of the main library for the officers' training programs. Although designed as temporary structures to last only for the duration of the war, some of these "T-buildings" were still standing fifty years later. The last of them were demolished to make way for the new Doe

Library stacks in the early 1990s. The military programs allowed the university to maintain something approaching its prewar enrollment. Nevertheless, the number of civilian male students declined from more than 11,000 before the war to about 4,300 in 1945. The campus went on a year-around academic schedule to help students finish their degrees before being drafted. Emeritus professors were called out of retirement to replace younger faculty who left for military service. Interscholastic athletics continued on a reduced scale, with teams often manned by large numbers of navy trainees. But many of the university's traditional rivals, including Stanford, suspended their athletic programs. As a result, the Cal football schedule included games with service teams like the Fleet City Marines and St. Mary's Pre-flight.

WARTIME BOOM

As important as military personnel were to the university's student body, the great bulk of new residents coming to Berkeley during the war years were civilians attracted by the new jobs generated by the Bay Area's overheated wartime economy. The federal government poured billions of dollars into the region, making the Depression-era public-works projects look paltry by comparison. West Berkeley industry boomed, with the military buying everything from Colgate toothpaste and Heinz ketchup to Cutter Lab blood plasma and Pacific Steel industrial castings.

Shipbuilding experienced the greatest expansion. In 1939 Bay Area shipyards had recovered from the depths of the Depression and employed about 5,000 workers. By 1944 the regional shipyard labor force numbered more than 240,000, nearly fifty times what it had been just five years earlier. The Bay Area had become the greatest shipbuilding center the world has ever seen, before or since. Old-time established yards saw huge increases in their workforce; Moore Drydock on the Oakland Estuary, for example, grew from about 600 employees in 1939 to 35,000 in 1944. The government also created brand-new "instant shipyards," including Henry J. Kaiser's massive industrial complex in Richmond. In 1940 the Kaiser Richmond yards did not exist: by 1943 they employed 100,000 workers, more people than had worked in the entire American shipbuilding industry in 1939.

The Bay Area's wartime production boom came at a time when ten to twelve million Americans were in the armed forces. The big labor surplus of the Depression years turned into a dramatic labor shortage almost overnight. Just about anyone who could stand upright for eight hours a day could get a job in the Bay Area during World War II. Shipyards and other East Bay employers encouraged elderly workers to come out of retirement and young students to enter the labor market. Katherine Archibald, a Cal sociology student, used her experience working at Moore Drydock as the basis for her classic book *Wartime Shipyard*. Berkeley High administrators were concerned about the numbers of young people dropping out of school to take well-paying shipyard jobs. The yards also made substantial efforts to recruit women workers: by 1945, about 25 percent of the blue-collar workers at Kaiser were women. Other employers were forced to follow suit. In 1943, for example, Colgate-Palmolive's West Berkeley plant announced that it had hired thirteen women to take jobs formerly held by men.

Even with all these nontraditional workers, Bay Area firms could not come close to meeting their labor needs. Large employers like Kaiser began nationwide recruiting campaigns to encourage workers to move to the region. The efforts were spectacularly successful, and new residents poured into the area, increasing the regional population by nearly a third during the war years. Included in the overall migration was the first large-scale influx of African Americans to the Bay Area. During the war years, the East Bay's black population increased from about four-teen thousand to sixty thousand. By 1945 nearly 70 percent of the African American wage earners in the Bay Area worked in just one industry—shipbuilding.

While there were no shipbuilding facilities in Berkeley, city residents had easy access to the largest East Bay employers. Long-established transit routes linked Berkeley to Moore Drydock and other yards on the Oakland Estuary. The Key System laid new tracks on San Pablo Avenue and Cutting Boulevard to provide service to the Kaiser complex in Richmond. The new Shipyard Line featured ancient cars that had once run on the New York elevated system. These transit connections made Berkeley a convenient place of residence for war workers. Landlords found more than enough tenants to make up for the enrollment declines at the university. Unfortunately for the landlords, however, apartments were subject to strict rent control, part of an extensive government wartime economic regime that included wage and price controls and the rationing of many goods and services, including gasoline.

AFRICAN AMERICAN MIGRATION

Berkeley was particularly affected by the African American migration, the city's black population growing from three thousand to more than twelve thousand between 1940 and 1945. Although Berkeley's black heritage goes back to the arrival of Pete and Hannah Byrne in 1859, the African American population remained small for the rest of the nineteenth century. In 1900 there were only sixty-six black residents in Berkeley. Oakland, by contrast, already had an African American population of more than one thousand. As the terminus for the transcontinental railroad, Oakland had an established black community that included sleeping-car porters, cooks, waiters, and others working in railroad occupations traditionally occupied by African Americans. But after the turn of the century, black professionals and prosperous blue-collar workers began to settle in Berkeley. In spite of the overall climate of discrimination, Berkeley had a reputation for relative tolerance. In South Berkeley, blacks could buy inexpensive homes in well-kept mixed neighborhoods. The African American population steadily increased, to five hundred in 1920, two thousand in 1930, and three thousand in 1940. By the beginning of World War II, Oakland and San Francisco had more black residents than Berkeley, but among Bay Area cities, Berkeley had the highest proportion of African Americans in its population—about 4 percent.

Blacks also had a small but growing presence at the university. The first African American graduate was Vivian Logan Rogers, who received her diploma in 1909. By the 1920s, black enrollment was large enough to support African American sororities and fraternities. They served as important social and political networks for the students. Although the organizations could not afford their own houses, they had contacts with black families with whom students could live and black business owners who had part-time jobs available. Both Stiles Hall and the University YWCA allowed African American students to use their facilities, and, after its opening in 1930, the International House welcomed blacks to its social and cultural activities.

During the thirties, black students joined with sympathetic whites to protest various forms of discrimination. Campus blacks also allied with community groups to boycott Berkeley businesses that refused to hire African Americans, campaigning on the slogan "Don't Buy Where You Can't Work." The students kept in touch with black community leaders like the attorney Walter Gordon, the Sleeping Car Porters Union vice president C. L. Dellums, and the political activist Frances Albrier. Albrier was an important figure in Berkeley life for more than three decades and in

1939 became the first African American to run (unsuccessfully) for the city council.

The great World War II migration both energized and overwhelmed the established black leadership. The huge increase in the black population gave the leadership a larger power base, and good wages earned in the shipyards provided greater economic security than the Berkeley black community had ever known. But new residents were not always willing to defer to the old leaders and did not fit comfortably into the web of close personal and family ties that characterized the old black community. Nevertheless, members of both groups joined in battles against various forms of discrimination and segregation, including the Jim Crow practices of the Boilermakers Union, the chief collective-bargaining agent for the shipyard workers. During the war years, black leaders in Berkeley joined the national "Double V" campaign, representing V for victory against fascism abroad and V for victory against racism at home.

HOUSING CRUNCH

With the wartime population influx, the region as a whole faced a serious housing shortage, but the situation was particularly bad for African Americans because there were so few neighborhoods in which they could live. One such neighborhood was South Berkeley. Ironically, the Japanese internment made more housing available just as the migration of war workers began. Nevertheless, the neighborhood soon became desperately overcrowded. Whole families were living in rented garages, and single workers were sharing beds. Since the shipyards operated twenty-four hours a day, on three eight-hour shifts, one person could sleep in the shared bed while another worked.

Another option for both blacks and whites was to apply for a unit in one of the several Bay Area wartime public housing projects. In San Francisco, Oakland, and Richmond, as elsewhere in the country, the federal government provided the funding, and the project was managed by a local city housing authority. Federal officials proposed a similar arrangement for Berkeley, asking the city to do its part to meet the regional housing crisis. African American and labor spokesmen favored the proposal, but the city council refused to cooperate, arguing that the units would attract "undesirable elements" and were inappropriate for a city consisting largely of single-family homes. After months of fruitless negotiations, the government took the unusual step of building and operating a Berkeley project without local participation. The result was Codornices Village, a complex of barrack-like apartments located west of San Pablo Avenue along Codornices Creek and straddling the Berkeley-Albany city line.

As was the case in most East Bay projects, about 25 percent of Codornices Village units were reserved for black families, who were placed in segregated housing blocks within the larger project. After the war, however, the percentage limits and segregation policies ended, and African Americans eventually became a majority among Codornices Village residents. Blacks were particularly affected by the rapid postwar decline in shipyard employment and the end of federal wartime policies that banned discrimination on defense contracts. As old patterns of job discrimination returned, blacks were more likely to need and qualify for public housing than whites. However, married university students, many subsisting on GI Bill benefits, also made up a significant portion of postwar Codornices Village tenants.

When the wartime emergency ended, federal officials argued they had no further authority to operate the project and again asked the city to accept responsibility. But Berkeley (and Albany) still refused to cooperate, and in 1955, after more than a decade of controversy, the feds finally closed Codornices Village. The Albany portion of the project was on UC property, and the university has continued to operate it as Albany Village, a housing complex for married students. Some of the original 1943 "temporary" buildings are still in use. The Berkeley section of the project was returned to private ownership and the property used for a number of nonresidential purposes. The African American residents were left high and dry, many of them forced to leave the city and seek low-cost housing elsewhere.

In spite of such discouraging developments, World War II improved many aspects of race relations in Berkeley and the nation as a whole. The internal migrations of war workers changed the demographics of cities like Berkeley, giving blacks a far greater role in community life. Migration out of the Jim Crow South and into Northern and Western cities also resulted in a large increase in the number of African American voters, thus increasing black political influence. Finally, the war changed the discourse on race. In the 1930s, the fight against racism was very much a matter of debate, even in liberal cities like Berkeley. But World War II definitively equated racism with fascism and identified the struggle against discrimination with the triumph of democracy. By the end of the war, "equal opportunity without regard to race" was considered a national principle, and postwar America was about to be asked to put its money where its mouth was on this matter. In the meantime, as one female African American war worker put it, "It was Hitler that got us out of white folks' kitchens."

THE ATOMIC AGE

As important as the shipyards and the labor migrations were, the most significant historical events in the Bay Area during the war years occurred in laboratories in the hills above the Berkeley campus. It was there and in Los Alamos, New Mexico, that Berkeley scientists led the world into the atomic age. Berkeley's part in this drama began in 1928, when the UC physics department recruited two promising young scientists to the faculty. Ernest O. Lawrence was an experimental physicist who, soon after arriving at Cal, began work on the cyclotron, a device that allowed revolutionary advances in the study of the atomic nucleus. When it appeared that Northwestern University might hire Lawrence away from Berkeley in 1930, President Sproul intervened in the tenure process to give the twenty-nine-year-old researcher a full professorship and a $1,200 a year raise. Sproul also helped obtain private funds from the Crocker family to support Lawrence's work and authorized the establishment of the Berkeley Radiation Laboratory in a ramshackle wooden building that dated from the 1880s. Lawrence more than repaid Sproul's support and confidence. In 1939 he became the first UC faculty member to win the Nobel Prize (and the first Berkeley resident to appear on the cover of *Time* magazine).

The other 1928 recruit, J. Robert Oppenheimer, was not nearly as well known to the public or, for that matter, to Sproul. But by the late 1930s, Oppenheimer's reputation among scientists was very high indeed. A theoretical physicist of great imagination and philosophical breadth, Oppenheimer was all but idolized by a group of promising graduate students who had gathered around him. The combination of Lawrence and Oppenheimer attracted some of the finest young scientific minds to Berkeley. It is hardly surprising, then, that the university played a key role in the Manhattan Project, the program to develop the world's first atomic weapons.

On the day before the Japanese attacked Pearl Harbor, Lawrence was at a meeting in Washington, where he was informed that the Manhattan Project had received presidential approval.

A few weeks later, Oppenheimer convened a small seminar in LeConte Hall on the UC campus to study the practical problems involved in building the atomic bomb. The federal government allocated funds for a vast expansion of Lawrence's radiation laboratory, allowing its relocation to the current site in the hills above campus. Among the lab's accomplishments was the production of the uranium-235 that fueled the bomb dropped on Hiroshima. The government also established another facility in Los Alamos, where the first bombs were developed and assembled. The Los Alamos lab was headed by Oppenheimer, the most important participant in the Manhattan Project.

The Berkeley lab was located on university property and directed and staffed by UC scientists. The staff of the Los Alamos facility included several Berkeley researchers in addition to Oppenheimer. It seemed reasonable, then, that the federal government should pay the university to manage the labs. In the early 1950s, when another Berkeley physicist, Edward Teller, established a third laboratory in Livermore to develop the hydrogen bomb, that lab also came under university management. (Teller needed a new facility in part because of his inability to work with the many Los Alamos scientists who disagreed with his conservative politics and his criticisms of Oppenheimer, who had opposed the H-bomb research.)

All three federal labs still exist and continue to be managed by the university. The Berkeley facility has not done classified weapons research in more than thirty years, but Livermore and Los Alamos remain the nation's nuclear weapons laboratories. In 2005, however, the federal government announced that, for the first time, it would put the labs' management contracts out to competitive bid. The Berkeley lab stayed under UC's wing, and the university made a successful bid to retain management of Los Alamos in partnership with the Bechtel Corporation. In 2007 the federal government also awarded the university a new management contract for the Livermore lab, again as part of a consortium including Bechtel. For more than sixty years, every item in the United States nuclear arsenal has been designed at a facility managed by the University of California.

The Manhattan Project completed the process begun in 1872, when Daniel Coit Gilman proposed that the new university devote itself primarily to scientific research. The university's role in developing atomic weapons also completed a process begun by Phoebe Apperson Hearst and Benjamin Ide Wheeler to make UC an institution of world renown. By the end of the 1940s, the world knew that Berkeley had given birth to the atomic age.

CHAPTER EIGHT

A KIND OF PEACE

On August 7, 1945, the United States destroyed most of the Japanese city of Hiroshima, dropping an atomic bomb fueled by uranium-235 made in Berkeley. Two days later another atomic weapon was dropped on Nagasaki. This time the bomb was fueled by plutonium, an element originally discovered in Berkeley by Glenn Seaborg and Edwin McMillan. Five days after the Nagasaki attack, on August 14, Japan surrendered, and World War II was over. In Berkeley, the *Daily Californian* put out a Peace Extra, and the Campanile bells played patriotic songs. Hundreds of students and residents paraded down Shattuck Avenue behind the university marching band. Car horns blared, and people threw firecrackers and confetti into the air. Some students lit a large bonfire on the streetcar tracks. But Berkeley's reaction was restrained compared to that of San Francisco. There drunken mobs staged a full-scale riot on Market Street, battling city and military police for hours before order was restored.

In spite of the public celebrations, many economists at UC and elsewhere feared that peace would bring a return to the high unemployment of the 1930s. Without the benefit of huge defense expenditures, they argued, the economy would never be able to absorb the millions of war veterans who were returning to the labor market. As it turned out, these fears never materialized. Wartime rationing and shortages produced a huge backlog of consumer demand, and a surge in household spending after the war eased the economic transition. Low interest rates and low levels of consumer debt stimulated home construction and sales. The war promoted technological and structural improvements in the United States economy and left the country with few international competitors whose economies were not damaged or destroyed. Government educational benefits contained in the GI Bill allowed colleges and universities rather than the labor force to absorb many of the veterans. Finally, almost as soon as military demobilization was completed, the United States began rearming to fight a cold war against the Soviet Union. The postwar period, then, was generally prosperous for the nation as a whole and for California in particular. It was an era of "a kind of peace," a not-quite-wartime period that brought important social and political changes to the nation, changes that inevitably affected Berkeley and its university.

A CENTRAL CITY IN A SUBURBAN AGE

After the war, Americans moved in ever-greater numbers to the suburbs, establishing what one scholar has called "the Crabgrass Frontier." Between 1945 and 1970 the population of the nine-county Bay Area doubled, yet the old central cities, San Francisco and Oakland, actually lost population. While these cities contained more than half of all the people living in the Bay Area in 1940, they accounted for only about a quarter of the regional population in 1970. Berkeley was part of the Bay Area's urban core by 1945, but, unlike San Francisco and Oakland, it was able to maintain or even increase its population of about 115,000 during the next quarter century. Nevertheless, thousands of white, middle-, and upper-middle-class families left Berkeley for the suburban periphery.

The key to this suburban growth was a vast public investment in the automobile. Although the construction of the bridges across the bay cemented the victory of the automobile in Bay Area life, the Depression and wartime gas rationing delayed the full implications of that triumph. After the war, the automobile culture reigned supreme, and in 1947 California embarked on a massive freeway program. The federal government contributed to its development with the establishment of the interstate system in 1956. In Berkeley, the old Eastshore Highway became a freeway, eventually a segment of Interstate 80. The Highway 24 freeway in Contra Costa County particularly affected Berkeley by facilitating the commute through the Caldecott Tunnel from Orinda, Lafayette, Walnut Creek, and beyond. In the 1960s Walnut Creek's population grew from ten thousand to forty thousand, and many of those new residents were former Berkeleyans.

The suburban boom was also spurred by the policies of government housing agencies. Middle-class families found it easier to get low-interest FHA, VA, or Cal-Vet loans for suburban homes than for buying or upgrading housing in racially mixed urban neighborhoods. Until restrictive covenants were declared unconstitutional in 1948, the FHA actually encouraged them, and it was not until the Kennedy presidency in the 1960s that racial discrimination was outlawed in FHA loan programs. The overwhelmingly white postwar suburbs may have been the product of free-market forces, but they were heavily subsidized and supported by public funds and policies.

Much of the outmigration from Berkeley was balanced by a

continuing influx of African Americans. During the war, with full employment and good wages, black families accumulated some wealth, and after the conflict they were anxious to fulfill the American dream of home ownership. The Berkeley flatlands were still one of the few areas in the Bay Area where well-maintained, affordable houses were available to blacks. Some unscrupulous realtors engaged in "block busting," scaring whites into selling with the threat that their street would became predominantly minority, thereby reducing property values. Throughout the city's history, South and West Berkeley had been mixed neighborhoods, initially multinational immigrant areas and then multiethnic working-class districts. As late as the 1940s, most black and Asian Berkeleyans lived in such mixed neighborhoods, but by the 1950s the city was becoming increasingly segregated, with the hills and campus area remaining predominantly white and large parts of the flatlands becoming mainly African American. For the first time observers began talking about Berkeley's "ghettos." In 1940 more than 90 percent of the city's population was white, and less than 5 percent was black. By 1970, the white proportion had dropped to 65 percent, and the black population had grown to nearly 25 percent.

POSTWAR UNIVERSITY

Another source of new residents that offset the suburban outmigration was the growth of the university. The GI Bill, which provided World War II veterans with federal financial aid to attend college, began the era of mass higher education in America. For the first time in U.S. history, millions of men and women from poor and working-class backgrounds had the option of a college education. California, which had already established the nation's most extensive system of public higher education, was better prepared than most states to respond to the new demand. Between 1945 and 1948 Cal's enrollment more than doubled, to more than twenty-five thousand.

To cope with this unprecedented growth, the university began a massive construction program that included physical expansion of the campus into the South Campus neighborhood. Sproul Hall occupied the east side of what had once been a block of the Telegraph Avenue business district. Some years later, construction of Sproul Plaza, the new student union building, and Zellerbach Hall completed the incorporation of everything north of Bancroft Avenue, south of Hearst Avenue, and east of Fulton Street into the campus. Massive university dormitories, playing fields, and parking structures were subsequently built in the South Campus district. Telegraph Avenue increasingly became a commercial area for students and campus habitués rather than a shopping district for the entire neighborhood.

Meanwhile, in areas adjacent to the campus, property owners divided up single-family dwellings to create student rentals and tore down old homes to make way for hastily built apartments. The Berkeley songwriter Malvina Reynolds may have coined the phrase "ticky-tacky" to refer to suburban tract homes south of San Francisco, but the term applied equally well to much of the speculative housing slapped up around the campus in the postwar years. Sometimes called dingbats, the new apartments featured breezeways and ground-floor carports. Supported by narrow posts above the carport, the buildings were (and are) seismic disasters waiting to occur. Yet they appealed to postwar students seeking independence from both parental and university control.

It was ironic that just as the undergraduate enrollment soared, the university increasingly deemphasized undergraduate education. In 1938 the American Council on Education reported that in a survey of the number of distinguished departments at elite institutions, UC and Harvard had tied for first among American universities. Cal's prestige steadily increased after the war, in part because of its participation in the Manhattan Project. During the 1940s and 50s, seven more university faculty members received Nobel Prizes, reinforcing the institution's exalted image. But the reputation for eminence was based on scholarship and graduate programs rather than on undergraduate education. In seeking out new faculty members, departments evaluated candidates on the basis of their published research and their ability to attract government money and foundation grants. Many of the new faculty were in fact excellent teachers and committed to undergraduate education, but that was not why they were hired or why they received tenure. Departments even offered reduced undergraduate teaching loads to attract promising scholars. In large lower-division lecture classes, undergraduates usually had more contact with graduate teaching assistants than with tenure-track faculty.

THE POLITICS OF ANTICOMMUNISM

The most serious debates on campus, however, were not about educational policies and priorities but about politics. In 1940 the Board of Regents had prohibited the hiring of communist faculty members, but during the war the alliance with the Soviet Union had suppressed anticommunist crusades. With the rapid deterioration of American-Soviet relations into a state of cold war, anticommunism reemerged as a potent political force. Many industries, communities, and, for that matter, universities benefited from defense dollars spent in the name of anticommunism. Although Senator Joseph McCarthy of Wisconsin may have been the most reckless and irresponsible anticommunist politician, he was hardly unique. Long before McCarthy was a household name, the legislative committee headed by the California state senator Jack Tenney was making headlines by investigating alleged communist influence in high places.

One of those places was the Berkeley campus. In hearings held from 1946 to 1948, Tenney dredged up a number of cases of prewar leftist activism in Berkeley, including J. Robert Oppenheimer's support for liberal causes and contacts with Marxist friends and family members. Although no specific charges of disloyal activity were ever made against Oppenheimer, his prewar political associations were eventually used as justification for revoking his security clearance after he opposed the development of the hydrogen bomb.

The publicity generated by the Tenney Committee particularly concerned James Corley, the university's comptroller and chief Sacramento lobbyist. He suggested that the Regents require all university personnel to take an anticommunist loyalty oath as a way of deflecting some of the bad press and political flak caused by the Tenney hearings. President Sproul agreed and formally recommended the oath at a March 1949 meeting of the Regents. During the lunch break, a university attorney drafted specific language, and after lunch the Regents unanimously adopted the measure.

For Corley, Sproul, and most of the Regents, the loyalty oath was an uncontroversial public-relations gesture. But for much of the Berkeley (and UCLA) faculty, it represented a violation of First Amendment rights and a threat to academic freedom and tenure. Led by the distinguished psychology professor Edward Tolman, the Academic Senate urged the Regents to revoke or revise the oath, and the stage was set for a dramatic struggle over power and principle. For more than a year, Sproul and senior faculty members like Joel Hildebrand unsuccessfully attempted to find a compromise. In the end Sproul concluded it was better to abolish the oath than to provoke a faculty revolt. Governor Earl Warren, a loyal Cal alum and former classmate of Sproul, agreed, arguing that "a Communist would take the oath and laugh." But a slim majority of the Regents eventually voted to fire any employee who refused to sign.

Thirty-one faculty members, including Tolman, and several dozen other employees held out to the bitter end and were dismissed. They promptly sued, and in 1952 the California Supreme Court held that the university could not impose a loyalty oath different from that required of all other state employees. Tolman and his colleagues were reinstated, but in the meantime the legislature had passed the Levering Act, which required all state workers to take an oath. In 1967 the U.S. Supreme Court finally ruled the Levering Act unconstitutional, and after eighteen years of campus controversy, matters were right back where they had been in 1949 when Corley first raised the issue. Meanwhile, on the Berkeley campus, the Regents had approved construction of Tolman Hall, a new education and psychology building named in honor of Edward Tolman.

The politics of anticommunism affected the city as well as the university. Berkeley public-school teachers, for example, also had to take the Levering oath. When the school board, after much debate, allowed the Marxist singer and actor Paul Robeson to perform in the new Berkeley Community Theater, the matter became a major issue in the next city election. Doris Walker, a Boalt Hall graduate who eventually became a prominent Bay Area attorney, was fired from a clerical job at Cutter Laboratories because of her leftist political beliefs. Her union, the International Longshoremen's and Warehousemen's Union, took her case all the way to the U.S. Supreme Court, but the justices let the firing stand. The ILWU itself was kicked out of the Congress of Industrial Organizations (CIO) because of charges of communist infiltration.

In spite of the dominant anticommunist mood, Berkeley leftists had some important local institutional power bases of their

FIGURE 24. Pacifist Lewis Hill founded KPFA in 1949. KPFA Radio & the Pacifica Foundation, Inc.

own. In 1949 KPFA went on the air as America's first listener-sponsored radio station. Although financial problems caused a temporary shutdown in 1951, the station recovered and has been in operation ever since. Founded by the pacifist Lewis Hill, KPFA was open to a remarkably wide range of perspectives and during the 1950s was often a lonely outlet for leftist viewpoints. Another institution with a leftist heritage, the Berkeley Consumer Cooperative, thrived after the war. It built a large supermarket on Shattuck Avenue in North Berkeley and established an active consumer education program. In 1962 the Co-op bought out the Sid's supermarket chain and transformed the large Sid's store on Telegraph Avenue into another Co-op market. In the 1970s it established additional stores in El Cerrito, Oakland, and Marin County. During the seventies, the Co-op operated three supermarkets in Berkeley, along with a pharmacy, bookstore, garage, hardware store, and credit union. A low Co-op membership number, indicating that you were among the original founders of the institution, was a prized status symbol in some Berkeley circles.

LIBERAL POLITICS

Although pro-business Republicans dominated Berkeley politics during the 1940s and 50s, demographic trends were working against them. Not only were largely Democratic black voters moving into the city, but it was often conservative whites who moved to the suburbs. Young, university-affiliated families who tended to vote Democratic often took their places. Liberal activists gravitated toward the Berkeley Democratic Club, which had been founded in 1934 to support Upton Sinclair's unsuccessful run for governor. In the fifties, the Berkeley club was affiliated with the liberal California Democratic Council, and Berkeley Democratic activists worked enthusiastically on Adlai Stevenson's presidential campaigns and Pat Brown's successful campaign for governor. In 1958, the same year that Brown defeated the stalwart East Bay Republican William Knowland, a liberal-labor coalition beat back a Knowland-supported state "right to work" initiative.

In Berkeley, liberals allied not only with labor but also with an increasingly politically active African American community. In the 1920s, the businessman D. G. Gibson had started the Appomattox Club as a way of organizing East Bay African Americans into a voting bloc. Like most blacks at the time, Gibson was a Republican, but growing African American support for Roosevelt and the New Deal moved him and his organization into the Democratic camp during the 1930s. The huge black population increase of the 1940s allowed Gibson to become something of a power broker. Black union members participated in the brief Oakland general strike of 1946 and were part of a liberal-labor group that unsuc-

cessfully attempted to gain control of the Oakland City Council
in 1947. In 1948 Gibson put together a coalition of CIO union
activists, white liberals, and African American voters to campaign
for the Sacramento Street pharmacist William Byron Rumford,
who was running for the state assembly in a district that included
much of Berkeley and part of Oakland. Rumford won the election,
becoming the first African American from Northern California to
serve in the legislature. He eventually authored the state's two most
important civil rights laws—the Fair Employment Practices Act
of 1959 and the Rumford Fair Housing Act of 1963.

By the mid-1950s, the liberal-labor–African American coalition
was ready to challenge the traditional Republican leadership of
Berkeley city government. Lionel Wilson, a future mayor of Oakland, received the Berkeley Democratic Club endorsement for a
seat on the Berkeley City Council. He didn't win, but white liberals like the city planning professor Jack Kent did. The labor
leader Jeffrey Cohelan became the first Democrat elected to Congress from Berkeley in decades. But the big Democratic break-
through came in 1961, when liberals finally won a majority on the
city council and school board and elected the first two African
American local office holders in Berkeley history: Wilmot Sweeney
to the council and Reverend Roy Nichols to the school board.

The new council majority immediately faced a major land-use
decision. At the turn of the century, a portion of Berkeley tidelands had been purchased by the Santa Fe Railroad for a right-
of-way that was never used. In 1913 the state granted Berkeley an
additional 7.32 square miles of San Francisco Bay that was shallow enough to fill. The city master plan, approved in the 1950s,
provided for the filling and development not only of the private
tidelands (most of which had already been filled), but also of the
city grant, which was still almost entirely open water. From the
point of view of the business-oriented city governments of the

1950s, the waterfront properties offered an opportunity for dramatic new growth and economic development.

However, three East Bay women, Catherine Kerr, Sylvia McLaughlin, and Esther Gulick, were concerned about the aesthetic and environmental impacts of the proposal. In the early sixties, they organized an ambitious grass-roots campaign to change the plan and greatly limit future bay fill and development. The new city council majority eventually agreed and limited future fill to what is now the Berkeley Marina (which was created from about forty years' worth of Berkeley garbage dumped into the bay). Most of the marina was planned as parkland and recreational facilities, with only a small portion devoted to restaurants and a hotel. On the basis of this success, Kerr, McLaughlin, and Gulick went on to organize the Save San Francisco Bay Association, which in 1965 brought about powerful state legislation strictly limiting fill and controlling shoreline development throughout the bay. By 2000, the former Santa Fe lands along the Berkeley waterfront west of the I-80 freeway were also preserved as open space, having been incorporated into the new Eastshore State Park created by legislation sponsored by the Berkeley assemblyman (and future mayor) Tom Bates. In another important land-use decision in the early 1960s, the liberal council majority joined Republican mayor Wallace Johnson in supporting a bond issue to keep the Berkeley BART line underground. The new rapid-transit system would thus not visibly divide East and West Berkeley as rail lines had in the past.

CIVIL RIGHTS POLITICS

Given the realities of Berkeley and national life in 1961, it was inevitable that the most dramatic actions of the new liberal majorities on the council and school board would involve race. The civil rights movement had existed in the South for more than five years, and the presence of segregation and discrimination in northern and western cities like Berkeley could no longer be ignored. In Berkeley, white liberal candidates had won black votes by promising to bring about measurable change. After taking office, the new city council appointed an eighteen-member citizens' committee to study the issue of housing discrimination. Not surprisingly, the committee found such discrimination endemic and called for a strong local ordinance outlawing the practice. After a number of contentious meetings, the council passed a tough law that included criminal penalties for those guilty of discrimination.

The opposition immediately began collecting signatures to bring the matter before the voters in a 1963 referendum. In just three weeks they collected more than three times the number of signatures needed. Most of the referendum supporters argued that the fair-housing law violated basic property rights, some advocates even claiming that it smacked of communism. A few of the referendum proponents specifically raised the issue of race. One man asserted that the housing law was "a plot to Congo-lize our city," and a Thousand Oaks neighborhood realtor said, "The day I have to sell to a Negro and ruin this fine district, I'll close up and get out of the real estate business."

By a small margin, the voters passed the referendum and thus overturned the law. In the same election, the Republican mayoral candidate, Wallace Johnson, who favored the referendum, narrowly defeated the liberal Democrat Fred Stripp, who opposed it. A few months later Byron Rumford got a more moderate fair-housing law through the California legislature. After Governor Brown signed the measure, the California real-estate industry sponsored a statewide initiative to overturn it. Ironically, in that election, Berkeley voters chose to support the Rumford Act and turn down the initiative, while the California electorate as a whole supported the initiative and turned down the act. The final chapter was written by the U.S. Supreme Court, which ruled the initiative unconstitutional in 1967. Thus the Rumford Act was reinstated and is still in force.

Not to be outdone by the city council, the new school board took on the even more explosive issue of school segregation. By 1961 school enrollments reflected the racial pattern of housing in Berkeley. Flatland elementary schools, particularly in South Berkeley, had predominantly black student bodies, while the hill schools were virtually all white. Garfield Junior High in North Berkeley was overwhelmingly white, while Burbank on University Avenue was largely black. Willard Middle School on Telegraph Avenue was ethnically mixed, as was Jefferson Elementary School in North Berkeley. But these two institutions were unusual: most Berkeley kids went to largely segregated schools until they reached Berkeley High. Even there, ability tracking often kept racial groups in separate classrooms. While the courts were slowly enforcing the 1954 Supreme Court *Brown v. Board of Education* decision, outlawing educational segregation in the South, schools in northern and western cities like Berkeley were becoming ever more segregated. The fact that this segregation was de facto, the result of residential patterns, rather than de jure, the result of discriminatory laws, made little difference to civil rights activists.

In 1964 Berkeley's liberal school board voted to desegregate the city's junior high schools by turning Burbank into a ninth-grade school for the entire city and distributing seventh- and eighth-graders to Garfield and Willard in a racially balanced matter. The city's daily newspaper, the conservative *Berkeley Gazette*, which had previously opposed the fair-housing law, claimed the school board was "destroying a city to test a theory." Some Garfield parents led a recall campaign against board members who supported the plan. Although the campaign lacked the overtly racist rhetoric of the fair-housing debate, emotions were high on both sides. The future of Berkeley's children seemed at stake. In the end voters over-whelmingly rejected the recall, and the board took that as a mandate to proceed with elementary-school desegregation.

Under the leadership of school superintendent Neil Sullivan, voluntary elementary desegregation was instituted in 1966, and a large citizens' committee began studying the possibility of a mandatory plan. In 1968 the board accepted the committee's recommendation to put such a plan into effect. It involved two-way busing, with black children being transported to hill schools and white children transported to flatland schools. In the fall of 1968 Berkeley became the only city in the nation to institute comprehensive two-way elementary-school busing for desegregation purposes without a court order requiring it.

In one form or another, the two-way busing program remained in effect for more than twenty-five years. It was not substantially altered until the 1990s. The results were mixed: it did not bring the end of all racial barriers and hostilities that the most idealistic supporters had hoped for, and it certainly did not close the educational achievement gap between white and black students. But desegregation also did not cause the destruction of the school system and produce an overall decline in student achievement, as the most determined opponents had feared.

If nothing more had happened in Berkeley in the 1960s than the fight over fair housing and the attempt to desegregate the schools, the city would still have attracted considerable national attention. Indeed, both stories made it into the *New York Times* and onto Walter Cronkite's *CBS Evening News*. But of course far more was happening in Berkeley during that decade. The city gave birth to a social and cultural rebellion that, for better or worse, came to define much of what "the sixties" was all about.

CHAPTER NINE

THE HERITAGE OF THE SIXTIES

The mainstream of American politics is moderate to conservative, but the United States also has an important tradition of home-grown radicalism. Episodic rather than ideological, American radicalism usually appears attached to some great cause, such as abolition, women's suffrage, trade union organization, or pacifism. Never dominant in these movements, the radical tradition has nevertheless profoundly affected them and occasionally profoundly affected the society and culture as a whole. Such was the case during the sixties, actually a decade stretching from about 1964 to 1974, when the issues of racial justice and the Vietnam War absorbed the nation. It was also an era of social and cultural rebellion against conformity and the establishment. No place was more affected by the politics and rebellions of these years than Berkeley. The city's reputation as "the People's Republic of Berserkeley" derives from this period and probably best expresses the common popular understanding (or misunderstanding) of the experience and heritage of Berkeley in the sixties.

THE ROOTS OF PROTEST

By the late 1950s, the concept of mass higher education had been well established, and middle-class students were arriving in Berkeley assuming that college education was a right rather than a privilege. Younger and less likely to be burdened with family responsibilities than the World War II veterans, the students of the late 1950s were virtually assured of a reasonably well-paid job on receipt of a Cal degree. They had more time for fun and games than the veterans, and in Berkeley the biggest single outpouring of student energy and emotion during the decade was a riotous panty raid on a hot spring evening in 1956.

But some students also had time for serious political and social concerns. The civil rights movement had begun in 1955, exposing a terrible social evil and setting a heroic example of change achieved through direct action and nonviolent civil disobedience. Questions about nuclear weapons development and America's support for right-wing dictatorships undermined some students' faith in anticommunism and the cold war. Professors often criticized the 1950s students for being a "silent generation" and urged them to speak out and become more politically involved. Much to the dismay of many of those same professors, some students were about to take that advice with a vengeance.

In 1957 activist students at Berkeley formed TASC, Toward an Active Student Community. The organization campaigned against racial segregation in student housing, opposed compulsory ROTC, and supported participatory educational projects that promoted social justice, world peace, and international understanding. Later in the year, TASC formed a new student political party, Slate, and ran a ticket of candidates in the Associated Students of the University of California election. In 1959 the party's candidate was elected student body president, and several

Slate members won seats on the ASUC executive committee. The party also began publishing the *Slate Supplement to the General Catalog*, which contained candid and often highly critical student evaluations of individual courses and professors. In 1962 Slate achieved one of its primary goals when the Board of Regents abolished compulsory ROTC on UC campuses.

At the same time, Berkeley students were becoming involved in off-campus causes. Cal undergrads, particularly residents of the Barrington Hall co-op on Dwight Way, were part of the crowd of demonstrators protesting against the San Francisco meeting of the House Committee on Un-American Activities in 1960. The committee hearings, held in City Hall, were designed to expose the nefarious deeds of alleged Bay Area communists, including two Berkeley public-school teachers. The KPFA commentator William Mandel was called to testify, and the committee found him something less than a friendly witness. "If you think for one minute I am going to cooperate with this collection of Judases, of men who sit here in violation of the Constitution," Mandel proclaimed, "if you think I will cooperate with you in any way, you are insane."

When the demonstrators were barred from the committee room, they began singing and chanting. San Francisco authorities turned on fire hoses and washed the protesters down City Hall's marble staircase before arresting them. Although a municipal judge later dismissed the criminal charges, the incident became notorious. Conservatives produced a film, *Operation Abolition*, which used newsreel footage of the demonstration and Mandel's testimony to show how Berkeley radicals were subverting the committee. Leftists answered with their own film, emphasizing the committee's reckless disregard for civil liberties.

In the early sixties Berkeley activists also participated in demonstrations against employment discrimination in the Bay Area. Huge protest rallies occurred along San Francisco's Auto Row, at

Fisherman's Wharf, and at the Palace Hotel. In Berkeley, demonstrators targeted the Lucky supermarket on Telegraph Avenue for a "shop-in." Protesters filled shopping carts to overflowing, but when clerks rang up the bill, the protesters politely walked away, explaining that they had no money. The tactic brought business to a standstill and helped persuade Lucky officials that it was time to hire minorities.

Clark Kerr, who succeeded Sproul as UC president in 1958, attempted to adjust to the era of increased activism by relaxing some rules governing campus political speech and activity. For example, political candidates were allowed to speak on campus for the first time since the 1930s, and Slate was permitted to sponsor an on-campus speech by Frank Wilkinson, a well-known southern California attorney and radical whom the House Committee on Un-American Activities had accused of being a communist.

The Kerr Directives, as the new rules were sometimes called, still prohibited most organizational political activity. Political groups could not raise money, solicit membership, or hold demonstrations or other events on university property. In keeping with tradition, students carried out many of these activities on city sidewalks at the edge of campus. In the 1930s, Sather Gate had been the natural location, but by the 1960s the campus had expanded a block farther south. Thus the sidewalk opposite the corner of Bancroft Way and Telegraph Avenue became the site of numerous card tables set up by students advocating various causes. In the summer of 1964, the *Oakland Tribune* publisher, William Knowland, complained that student groups were using the area to organize against the Republican presidential candidate, Barry Goldwater. Investigating the complaint, university officials discovered that the sidewalk was in fact part of the campus. (The Regents had voted to donate the area to the city, but the decision had never been carried out.)

THE FREE SPEECH MOVEMENT

When the students returned from summer vacation in September of 1964, they were confronted with notices informing them that the Kerr Directives would henceforth be enforced on the Bancroft Way sidewalk. Ironically, it was Clark Kerr who had originally recommended that the property be transferred to the city, but because the transfer hadn't occurred, the Berkeley chancellor, Edward Strong, and vice chancellor, Alex Sheriffs, insisted the rules be enforced. In response, a broad coalition of student groups, from Slate to the conservative Young Americans for Freedom, protested what they considered to be a violation of free speech. Leftist activists, including some who had spent the summer working with civil rights groups in the South, decided to use direct action and civil disobedience to oppose the administrative restrictions. They set up recruiting and organizing tables at Sather Gate and in Sproul Plaza, openly violating campus rules. The activists also transformed the structure of the protest from a "united front" of organizations to the Free Speech Movement (FSM), a separate group with its own identity and highly informal governing process.

On October 1, a former student, Jack Weinberg, sat down at an illegal table in front of Sproul Hall. When he refused to move, campus police officers arrested him and placed him in a police car. More than a hundred students then surrounded the car, refusing to let it move unless Weinberg was released. A standoff ensued, with Weinberg remaining in the car for thirty-two hours. The vehicle became an impromptu stage for a very extended rally. Late in the evening, students opposing FSM, including some members of the football team, began to heckle the speakers, and the nonviolent mood was only barely maintained. Finally, at about 7:30 P.M. the next day, a settlement was reached between the ad-

FIGURE 25. Jack Weinberg spent 32 hours in a police car on Sproul Plaza in October 1964. Bancroft Library, University of California, Berkeley.

ministration and FSM negotiators. Mario Savio, a philosophy major who had emerged as the leading FSM spokesman, climbed onto the roof of the police car and announced the agreement. He asked demonstrators "to rise quietly and with dignity and go home."

Any hope that the October 2 agreement had ended the conflict was dashed in November, when the university began issuing disciplinary suspensions of FSM leaders. Matters steadily deteriorated, and on December 2 the FSM held a sit-in at Sproul Hall. "There is a time," Mario Savio told his compatriots, "when the operation of the machine becomes so odious, makes you so sick at heart, that you can't take part; you can't tacitly take part, and you've got to put your bodies upon the gears and upon the wheels, upon the levers, upon all the apparatus and you've got to make it stop." With Joan Baez singing "We Shall Overcome," more than a thousand demonstrators filed into the building and prepared to occupy it for what turned out to be fifteen hours. Governor Pat Brown eventually ordered the building cleared, and at 3 A.M. on December 3 a six-hundred-strong force of campus and Berkeley police, Alameda County deputy sheriffs, and California Highway Patrol officers began carrying students out of Sproul Hall. It took nearly twelve hours to arrest all the demonstrators and put them in buses bound for Santa Rita County Jail. The remaining FSM leadership called a campus strike, and many professors and teaching assistants, particularly in the humanities and social sciences, canceled classes. Eight hundred faculty members gathered at an ad hoc meeting and called for an end to "the series of provocation and reprisal that has resulted in disaster."

On December 7, President Kerr called a university meeting in the Greek Theater to present a compromise solution crafted by a group of faculty department chairs. After Kerr finished his presentation, Mario Savio approached the stage to address the crowd but was physically blocked and hauled away by university police. The incident destroyed any goodwill that had been generated at the meeting, and the FSM rejected the compromise. Finally, on December 8, the Academic Senate overwhelmingly passed a resolution that suspended any past university disciplinary measures against the demonstrators and limited campus regulations on political activity to reasonable rules regarding the time, place, and manner. The content of events was no longer subject to university control. The FSM had won; the Kerr Directives were dead.

BROADENING THE CONTEXT

The Regents' somewhat grudging acceptance of the essence of the faculty resolution ended the Free Speech Movement and its on-campus struggle. (Some poorly attended "filthy speech" rallies received media attention for a few weeks in 1965.) Henceforth, significant Berkeley demonstrations would be linked to broad national and world issues rather than local campus concerns. Even during the fall of 1964, Savio and other FSM orators attempted to put their campus conflict into a broad context. From their perspective, the university's conduct was typical of the coercive corporate and public bureaucracies that dominated modern life. Campus radicals called for new participatory institutions that promoted creativity and humane values. These concerns paralleled those outlined in the earlier Port Huron Statement by the Students for a Democratic Society. But whereas the SDS paper was distributed to a few true believers, the FSM rhetoric, and thus the message of what was going to be called the "New Left," reached millions of TV viewers. The Berkeley activists were members of the first television generation, and they knew how to coin sound bites and time their rallies for maximum exposure on the evening news. Jack Weinberg's line, "Never trust anyone over thirty," was broadcast into living rooms across the country and became a sixties watchword.

National and world events seemed to confirm the activists' analysis. 1965 was the year of the Watts Rebellion, the first of the great urban upheavals of the late sixties. It symbolized a shift in the focus of the black protest movement from the rural South to

FIGURE 26. Bobby Seale and Huey P. Newton, founders of the Black Panther Party, 1967. Photo © Ted Streshinky/Corbis.

the urban North and West, as well as an end to strict adherence to nonviolent methods. In 1966 Huey P. Newton and Bobby Seale founded the Black Panther Party. Headquartered in South Berkeley and later in Oakland, the party remained a source of militant rhetoric and action for the rest of the decade. Seale, in particular, had Berkeley roots, having spent part of his childhood in the Codornices Village housing project.

Also taking place in 1965 was the Delano Strike, a walkout of Mexican and Filipino farm workers in the San Joaquin Valley. Berkeley sympathizers supported grape boycotts and formed auto convoys to transport supplies to the strikers. Delano made Cesar Chavez a national figure and a frequent participant in Berkeley events. The strike also promoted a new level of political activity and militancy among young Latinos. It was a sign that the black protest movement was broadening to include other groups and become what the sixties called a "Third World Movement." Young Asian Americans began a campaign to win monetary reparations for victims of the World War II internment. The American Indian Movement's 1969 occupation of Alcatraz signaled a new era of militant Native American protest activity. On the Berkeley campus, the Third World Liberation Front led militant demonstrations calling for ethnic studies programs and a "Third World College." The campaign failed to win the separate college but did lead to campus affirmative-action programs and the establishment of ethnic studies departments.

Above all, 1965 was the year that President Lyndon Johnson decided to send combat troops to Vietnam. The Vietnam conflict divided American society more profoundly than any event since the Civil War. To campus militants and their allies, Vietnam symbolized the establishment's militarism and racist imperialism. Male students were painfully aware that they faced the draft and possible combat in Vietnam if they lost their student deferments. Poor and minority Americans were usually ineligible for deferments and served in the military in disproportionate numbers. Berkeley was the location of one of the nation's first large protests against the war, in May 1965, when the Vietnam Day Committee sponsored a teach-in that attracted more than twenty thousand participants. Oakland police turned back two protest marches to the Oakland Army Base, the embarkation point for many of the troops serving in Vietnam. Some of the marchers were accosted by Hell's Angels who yelled, "Go back to Russia, you fucking communists!" Events in Southeast Asia continued to produce protest marches, rallies, and even violent demonstrations for the rest of the decade. More than anything else, Vietnam was the glue that held the various parts of the sixties protest movement together.

CULTURAL REBELLION

Along with political protest came a cultural or lifestyle rebellion. Some people of color rejected what they believed to be white, middle-class values and attempted to construct separate ethnic or third-world identities. Many young whites also sought alternatives to what they considered the repressive middle-class way of life of mainstream America. For some it was simply a chance for "sex and drugs and rock and roll," but for others it was a profound search for new forms of ecstatic and spiritual consciousness and new ways of expressing simple, youthful idealism. Berkeley, of course, had been fertile ground for "alternative lifestyles" since the early twentieth century. During the 1950s, when San Francisco was the unofficial capital of the Beat Generation, Berkeley was an important outpost of the movement, with the poets Allen Ginsberg, Gary Snyder, and Robert Duncan and the novelist Jack Kerouac at one time or another living in the city. The UC English professor Tom Parkinson was one of the first scholars to take Beat literature seriously. Similarly, in the 1960s, when San Francisco's Haight Ashbury neighborhood was the center of a new counterculture universe, Berkeley was again a closely orbiting satellite.

Perhaps nowhere did the political and cultural rebellions of the sixties come together more completely than in Berkeley. South of the UC campus were neighborhoods where activist students, counterculture street people, and black militants shared more or less adjoining turf. The area was dotted with communal living groups committed both to radical politics and to new social and cultural experiments. Telegraph Avenue became contested territory, claimed both by establishment merchants and police on the one hand, and the counterculture in all its guises on the other. By the late sixties, the focal point of demonstrations and violent confrontations had moved off campus and onto the Avenue. The counterculture established its own institutions, including new media. Max Scherr founded the *Berkeley Barb*, one of the first alternative newspapers, in 1965.

The greatest of all of Berkeley's sixties confrontations was over the control of an unimpressive lot located just east of Telegraph Avenue between Haste Street and Dwight Way, a patch of land that came to be known as People's Park. As part of its massive expansion into the South Campus neighborhood, the university purchased the property in the 1950s and cleared the existing buildings in 1968. The result was a muddy, trash-filled mess, used as an informal parking lot. In the spring of 1969, activists began discussing the idea of turning the area into a park. In April, the *Berkeley Barb* called on people to build "a cultural, political, freak out, and rap center for the Western World," adding, "We will police our own park and not allow its occupation by an imperial power."

This was not exactly what the university had in mind for the property, and before dawn on May 15, campus contractors had built a chain-link fence around the site. Later in the day, the ASUC president, Dan Siegel, urged spectators at a Sproul Plaza rally to "go down and take over the park." Some did, and all hell broke loose. Demonstrators battled Berkeley and campus police and Alameda County deputy sheriffs. One onlooker, James Rector, was killed by a sheriff's shotgun blast, and more than one hundred other people were injured. Governor Ronald Reagan called in the National Guard and placed Berkeley under military curfew. A few days later, a guard helicopter dropped a tear-gas bomb on a campus rally, and the wind blew the noxious fumes over parts of North Berkeley, forcing the closure of Oxford Elementary School.

Led by Pat and Fred Cody, owners of Cody's Books (located a couple of blocks from the contested property), some people of goodwill attempted to intervene between the counterculture and

FIGURE 27. National Guard troops in downtown Berkeley during the People's Park disturbances, 1969. Courtesy of the Berkeley Public Library, Berkeley, CA.

the establishment and bring about a peaceful conclusion to the May confrontations. The result was a giant Memorial Day march that attracted at least twenty-five thousand participants. The event was more a sixties love-in than a political protest. Marchers danced, sang, smoked dope, placed flowers in the barrels of guardsmen's rifles, and laid sod on Haste Street, symbolically reclaiming the pavement for the earth. The Codys and others also worked on the Telegraph Summer Program, which established a number of "free" institutions and programs to serve the community. (Some of the Avenue habitués were so used to living by their wits that they continued to steal items that were being given away at the Free Store.) One of the program's most important institutions, the Free Clinic, still exists more than thirty-five years after its founding. But these initiatives left the final status of People's

Park unsettled. It has been the subject of community conflict and the scene of occasional confrontations ever since.

THE TWILIGHT OF THE SIXTIES

The U.S. expansion of the Vietnam War into Cambodia in 1970 produced the last of the great Berkeley protests of the sixties. While periodic demonstrations and "trashings" occurred on Telegraph Avenue after 1970, none had the energy or large popular base of the great sixties rebellions. By the time that the Symbionese Liberation Army assassinated the Oakland school superintendent, Marcus Foster, and kidnapped Patricia Hearst (Phoebe's great-granddaughter) from her South Campus apartment in 1974, it seemed that some of the surviving elements of the New Left had lost touch with moral and political reality.

Many other former activists had gone on with their lives, raising families, starting careers, and, in effect, rejoining the great American middle class. They often continued their commitment to social change through careers in teaching and other forms of public service. Some sixties veterans left the city for rural communes, and still others burned out on the excesses of the counterculture lifestyle. Some were also victims of political repression, including the FBI's infamous COINTEL program. The winding down of the war and the end of the draft, as well as the adoption of New Left ideas by establishment politicians like George Mc-Govern, took more wind out of the movement's sails. Ultimately, the cultural rebellion of the sixties may have had a greater social impact than its political radicalism. For better or worse, sex and drugs and rock and roll were well adapted to the realities of the great American marketplace and profoundly affected mainstream cultural values and practices.

The most important California political figure produced by the sixties was not a movement participant like Tom Hayden but Ronald Reagan, a very conservative Republican. Reagan's role as leader of the backlash against the activism and rebellion of the era, including what he called "the mess in Berkeley," helped propel him into the governor's office in 1966 and eventually to the White House in 1980. In spite of their vehement dislike for each other, Reagan and the Berkeley activists shared at least one common antagonist: liberal UC President Clark Kerr.

Thanks to the efforts of the journalist Seth Rosenfeld, we know that the FBI director, J. Edgar Hoover, profoundly influenced Reagan's attitudes toward Kerr. Beginning as a student reporter for the *Daily Californian* and continuing as a writer for the *San Francisco Examiner* and *San Francisco Chronicle*, Rosenfeld waged a seventeen-year battle to obtain documents regarding the FBI's activities on and about the UC campus. He found that throughout the cold war, the bureau had informants in Berkeley and kept dossiers on a number of campus personalities.

Hoover disliked Kerr's liberal politics and apparently blamed him for an essay assignment for entering students that portrayed the FBI in an unfavorable light. Like most conservatives, Hoover believed Kerr had seriously mishandled the FSM upheavals. Shortly after he took office as governor, FBI agents briefed Ronald Reagan on these matters. Hoover also discussed Kerr with the former CIA director John McCone, a Cal alumnus who passed on the FBI's concerns to members of the Board of Regents. On campus, the anti-Kerr campaign was promoted by some conservative faculty and staff members, including the psychology professor Hardin Jones and vice chancellor Alex Sheriffs (who subsequently served as Reagan's educational adviser). In 1967 Reagan engineered Kerr's dismissal, ironically on the grounds that the president had "coddled" the very student activists who had fought against the Kerr Directives and condemned Kerr's concept of a "multiversity." Years later, when UC took control of the former School for the Deaf and Blind site on Waring Street, the Board of Regents honored the man they had previously fired by officially naming the complex the Clark Kerr Campus.

THE HERITAGE OF THE SIXTIES

The New Left increased the political influence of people of color and inspired important social and cultural movements, including new expressions of feminist and environmental activism and liberation movements for gays and disabled people. The latter had a particular Berkeley dimension, with the founding of the Center for Independent Living by the disability activists Ed Roberts and Phil Draper in 1972. The center eventually moved into the old Cunha Pontiac building on Telegraph Avenue and became one of the largest and most influential disability service and advocacy groups in the country. But while these spin-offs of sixties activism were important, the New Left as a whole did not survive as an organized movement or a coherent political force. Perhaps its original anti-institutional bias and its reliance on moral indignation rather than pragmatic coalition-building doomed it as an ongoing organizational entity.

Except in Berkeley. Berkeley was indeed the exception that proved the rule, for it was in Berkeley that the New Left established an institutionalized presence and became a significant part of the political landscape. Liberal politicians had long urged campus and city radicals to pursue their goals through electoral politics rather than direct action. Much to the liberals' dismay, some activists accepted the suggestion in 1966, running the graduate student (and future journalist) Robert Scheer for congress. Scheer's opponent was not a conservative Republican but the incumbent Democrat, Jeffrey Cohelan, a liberal who nonetheless supported

Lyndon Johnson's policy in Vietnam. Although Cohelan survived the challenge, Scheer polled 40 percent of the votes in the Democratic primary, including a majority of the votes cast in the Berkeley portion of the congressional district. Cohelan was clearly vulnerable, as the city councilor Ron Dellums proved in 1970. Combining the votes of the Berkeley Left with solid support from the African American community, Dellums defeated Cohelan in the 1970 primary and went on to win the general election. In 1971 Dellums began a twenty-seven-year career as the most radical member of the U.S. House of Representatives.

The Dellums victory encouraged the Left to enter city politics with new energy. In 1971 three members of the leftist April Coalition slate won city-council seats. Although two of them were subsequently recalled, the 1971 election established the Left as a force in the local power structure. In 1973 traditional liberals and business conservatives buried the hatchet and formed a unified slate to oppose the Left. For the next decade, Berkeley politics were dominated by what amounted to two local parties almost completely unrelated to national partisan organizations. The support for each local party began at the city's liberal center, with "progressives," institutionalized as the Berkeley Citizens' Action, attracting votes to the left of that mark, and "moderates," variously known as the All-Berkeley Coalition or the Berkeley Democratic Club, picking up votes on the right. The electorate was fairly evenly split between the factions, with African Americans being the major swing vote. This division encouraged both groups to include black candidates on their slates, thus dramatically increasing the clout of black voters. Between 1973 and 1986, no one was elected to local office in Berkeley who was not endorsed by one of the two local parties.

For most of this period, moderates controlled the city council, but progressives set the political agenda with a series of controversial ballot initiatives. In 1973, for example, voters supported a measure that created a strong civilian police-review board. In the same year, voters also favored the Neighborhood Preservation Ordinance, which substantially slowed "ticky-tacky" development in residential areas. The new preservationist consciousness was also reflected in the passage of a Landmark Preservation Ordinance and the establishment of the Berkeley Architectural Heritage Association and the Berkeley Historical Society. Both groups honored (and sometimes idealized) the city's historic commitment to a special sense of civic consciousness and quality of life.

In the early eighties, at the suggestion of the rent-control activist Marty Schiffenbauer, the BCA managed to get the timing of city elections changed from April of odd-numbered years to November of even-numbered years, coinciding with state and national elections. This change increased student voter turnout, and in 1984 the leftist mayor Gus Newport and his allies captured eight of the nine council seats. In 1986 the moderates retaliated with a charter amendment that returned the city to district or ward elections for council for the first time since the turn of the century. The effect was to restore the close balance of power between the factions on the council but reduce African American representation on the body. For the next eight years, the progressive Loni Hancock served as mayor, as part of a narrow leftist majority.

RENT CONTROL

The most controversial issue in these years was rent control. During and immediately after World War II, Berkeley housing was covered by federal price controls on rents. Even when the controls expired, substantial apartment construction kept up with the housing demand, and rents remained relatively low. But by the seventies, residential down-zoning and the Neighborhood Preservation Ordinance combined with a poor business climate to slow new housing construction. The city's demography changed, with more single adults and couples and fewer families with children in the population, and this shift in turn created a greater demand for rental housing. Berkeley was also affected by a rapid rise in regional housing prices throughout the Bay Area. Finally, the university neglected to build new dormitory space to accommodate the steady increase in student numbers. The result of all these factors was skyrocketing rents and a growing demand by residents for relief. Because rentals made up about 60 percent of the city's individual housing units, the political impact of this protest was immense.

In the late 1970s the moderate city-council majority, which had substantial landlord support, was unwilling or unable to respond to the housing crisis. Housing activists therefore went directly to the electorate, and in 1980 the voters approved an initiative measure establishing rent control. The law was strengthened by subsequent initiatives, especially Measure G in 1982. Because the initiatives were written by rent-control advocates like Schiffenbauer, it is hardly surprising that each succeeding measure gave greater protection to renters. By the mid-eighties, Berkeley had some of the toughest rent-control policies in the nation.

Some landlords advocated civil disobedience, while others withdrew units from the rental market. In the end, property owners went over the city's head, fighting the rent-control laws in court and the state legislature. In the 1990s, the courts allowed landlords substantial rent increases and the legislature passed vacancy decontrol, allowing landlords to reset the rent each time a unit becomes vacant. Because of Berkeley's large, ever-changing student population, this decision dramatically reduced the clout of rent control.

What was striking about Berkeley's passionate debates over rent control in the 1980s and 90s was the extent to which both sides used arguments based on broad moral principle: the basic right to shelter versus the basic rights of property. It was as if rent control was an issue equivalent in moral weight to free speech, racial justice, or the Vietnam War. The transformation of often-mundane matters of local administration into issues of high moral principle is surely one of the legacies of the sixties.

In 2000 an attempt by the national Pacifica Foundation, the governing body of KPFA, to censor on-air content and fire some of the station's most popular commentators produced still another episode reminiscent of the sixties. KPFA listeners staged massive protests outside the station's studios on Martin Luther King Jr. Way and organized a popular "Save Pacifica" movement. In the end, the Pacifica management backed down, many of the board members and administrators leading the campaign resigned, and the network substantially changed its governing processes and structure. Nonviolent, direct action had won the day; the sixties spirit seemed alive and well.

Berkeley's enduring heritage of the sixties has promoted laudable popular involvement in community affairs and a willingness to defend important values and promote useful social experimentation. But it has also led to a self-righteous style of politics that sometimes gives greater weight to passion than to wisdom. In any case, it is clear that in Berkeley, the sixties are not quite over, the style and substance of that decade not quite old hat.

CHAPTER TEN

BERKELEY IN AN AGE OF INEQUALITY

In the early 1870s, Captain R. P. Thomas moved his Standard Soap Company from San Francisco to Ocean View. Thomas became one of Berkeley's most prominent residents and one of the first settlers in the Berkeley hills. His house was equipped with a cannon that he shot off each year to celebrate the Fourth of July. Thomas supported many civic improvements, including the first Berkeley–San Francisco ferry that ran briefly in the 1870s. But, most important, his Standard Soap Company provided jobs for several generations of working-class Berkeley residents.

The company was taken over by Peet Brothers in 1916 and subsequently absorbed into the Colgate-Palmolive Peet empire. In 1937 the International Longshoremen's and Warehousemen's Union organized employees at the Berkeley plant, and after World War II Colgate workers were among Berkeley's most militant union activists. They staged a major strike in 1952 and a ten-month-long walkout a decade later. During the latter dispute, the Berkeley workers promoted a national boycott of Colgate products, traveling around the country to drum up support for their cause. But union activism could not prevent the closing of the Colgate plant in the early 1980s. Although the ILWU negotiated severance packages for the workers, four hundred people lost well-paid union jobs when the facility closed in 1982.

THE DECLINE OF BLUE-COLLAR BERKELEY

The Colgate story was hardly unique. By the 1980s, dozens of the plants that had made up West Berkeley's industrial core had closed. They included the Heinz and Durkee food-processing facilities, the Hawes drinking-fountain factory, and the Manasse-Block tannery. In the early 1970s, leaders of the city's business community proposed a redevelopment project that would turn much of West Berkeley into an industrial park, but area residents successfully opposed such a radical reordering of their neighborhood. Instead, in 1993, after more than a decade of complex negotiations between various interests, the city council approved the West Berkeley Plan, an ambitious, multifaceted scheme that had as one of its major aims the preservation of Berkeley's industrial base and the lucrative blue-collar jobs it had produced. However, in the late 1990s the Colgate site still remained vacant, and the property's owners called the city's requirement that the site be reserved for traditional manufacturing purposes a "pipe dream." Instead, the owners asked that the West Berkeley Plan be amended to allow them to build a mixed-use research and residential structure.

Of course, Berkeley was hardly unique in losing traditional manufacturing jobs during the 1980s. The decline of smokestack industries was a nationwide phenomenon related to technological change and developments in the global economic system. In Berkeley and elsewhere, the new era produced winners and losers in a process that increased social and economic inequality. During the "protest decade" of the 1960s, young Berkeley activists had fought to achieve a more equitable society, but as they entered middle age, they found themselves living in an era of increased inequality. The decline of the well-paying, unionized, blue-collar jobs that had been created during and just after World War II was an important cause of this change.

It was not just that the poor were getting poorer; the rich were also getting richer. The Cal professor Robert Reich, secretary of labor in the Clinton administration, pointed out that the richest 1 percent of the population, in terms of income, held as much wealth as the bottom 90 percent. Such a level of inequality harked back to the Gilded Age of the late nineteenth century. In the early twenty-first century, the extraordinary cost of Bay Area housing exacerbated the problem. In Berkeley, only well-off professionals and business executives could afford houses in the hills. Middle-class professors, who once might have lived in hill neighborhoods, now bought homes in the formerly working-class flatlands. And university clerical and maintenance workers were nearly priced out of the housing market altogether. They were lucky to find affordable rentals.

The economic trends even negated some of the progress that had been made in civil rights. Although overt forms of racism and discrimination dramatically decreased, the economic gap between whites and some nonwhite groups increased. In spite of thirty years of school integration, a significant gap in average student achievement at Berkeley High still remained between whites and Asians on the one hand, and blacks and Latinos on the other. To the degree that educational success is closely related to economic mobility, the student achievement rates were discouraging news for Berkeleyans committed to a more equitable society. In 2002 the school board agreed to consider dividing Berkeley High into a number of small subschools within the common campus as a way of responding to some of the grave educational and administrative problems at the institution. By 2007 about half the students were enrolled in the subschools.

THE TRANSFORMATION OF WEST BERKELEY

The city's West Berkeley Plan did protect some small industrial enterprises and promoted the presence of art and craft studios in the area. In addition, some of West Berkeley's traditional manufacturing companies survived, including the Macaulay Foundry and the Pacific Steel Casting Company. Perhaps the greatest success was the preservation of the former Cutter Laboratories. Established in 1903, Cutter became a major producer of medical products, including a popular line of insect repellents. As at Colgate, its workers were organized by the ILWU, and by the 1980s, Cutter was Berkeley's largest unionized private employer. In 1984 the firm was bought out by Miles Laboratories, which was subsequently absorbed into the Bayer pharmaceutical empire. By this time, the Bay Area had emerged as the world's leading center of biotechnical research and development, largely because of the presence of the region's universities. In the East Bay, Chiron Corporation in Emeryville anchored a complex of regional biotech firms, many of which, like Chiron, were started by UC scientists.

To take advantage of this invaluable commercial and intellectual network, Bayer wanted to transform the old Cutter facility into the corporation's worldwide biotechnical center. To facilitate the transformation, Bayer asked the city for substantial zoning changes to allow for the physical growth of the company's West Berkeley site. In 1991 the city approved the changes after Bayer agreed to a number of ameliorative measures. By the end of the 1990s, the workforce at the former Cutter facility had grown to more than five hundred unionized employees.

The Cutter-Bayer story was unusual in two respects. The company was the only old West Berkeley manufacturing enterprise to make a smooth transition into the new age of high-tech industry, and it was Berkeley's only major high-tech employer with a unionized workforce. Berkeley's other biotech companies and its numerous computer-software enterprises were solidly non-union. In the 1980s and 90s, Berkeley's economy generated new employment that more than made up for the traditional manufacturing jobs that had been lost, but most of the new jobs were no longer positions that offered good wages to blue-collar workers with limited education. Even technician and production-line jobs in the new industries demanded substantial education and training. One of the ameliorative measures Bayer agreed to was financial support for an educational program at Berkeley High and Vista Community College to prepare Berkeley students for careers as technicians in biotech. Vista eventually pulled out of the effort, however, when the college biotech faculty concluded that the program would not give students sufficient educational background for anything but low-level employment.

THE NEW ECONOMY

If many traditional manufacturing jobs disappeared, employment in cultural and artistic occupations boomed. The city gave rise to a significant visual arts scene, and the presence of the university assured that Berkeley would be a center of classical music composition and performance. A thriving music program in the public schools helped Berkeley produce a generation of talented jazz performers, and the city's countercultural heritage nurtured a strong local tradition of experimental rock music.

Using profits largely gained from the success of a local band, Creedence Clearwater Revival, Fantasy Records expanded into film production in the 1970s. Headquartered in a large building that loomed over its West Berkeley neighbors, Fantasy produced such notable movies as *One Flew Over the Cuckoo's Nest*, *Amadeus*, and *The English Patient*. Hollywood awarded Fantasy's owner, Saul Zaentz, an Oscar for lifetime achievement in 1997. But in Berkeley his greatest influence may have been his practice of renting out office space and production facilities to local filmmakers, which made the city into a center of documentary video and film production. Zaentz's retirement and Fantasy's closing, announced in 2004, could dramatically affect local filmmaking and thus the city's economy.

Berkeley book publishing also thrived. The University of California Press grew into one of the largest scholarly publishing houses in the nation and, beginning with Theodora Kroeber's *Ishi in Two Worlds* in 1961, also entered the general book market with some success. The area's progressive climate nurtured a number of additional lively publishing ventures, including Heyday Books and such specialty presses as Ten Speed, Nolo, and Shambhala (now based in Boston). The collectively owned and managed Book People, headquartered in West Berkeley, became a major national distributor of works produced by independent publishers. And publishers and distributors were only part of the lively Berkeley literary scene, which included a remarkable number of published authors (including the Pulitzer Prize winner Michael Chabon) and one of the finest selections of bookstores in the country. If literary and artistic occupations often provided little monetary compensation, they nourished and enriched the city's spirit and gave sustenance to its soul.

Many of the other new jobs created in Berkeley during the 1980s and 90s were in what might be called the yuppie service sector. The word *yuppie*, referring to young urban professionals, was coined in the early eighties by the Berkeley writer Alice Kahn in a wry social commentary published in the *East Bay Express*. Although the national media quickly adopted the word, it was particularly applicable to Berkeley. College-educated people in their twenties and thirties were moving to Berkeley, attracted by the cultural life of the university town and the relatively tolerant, multiethnic environment. Living costs were somewhat lower than San Francisco, and the new residents often held good jobs or at least had good job prospects. Often childless and with few other family obligations, the young professionals had money to spend on good food, drink, and other pleasures. This affluence created opportunities for a new generation of Berkeley entrepreneurs, often veterans of the cultural wars of the sixties. They responded to the yuppie market with a wide array of new businesses, ranging from coffeehouses to New Age boutiques.

Prominent among the new Berkeley business owners was Alice Waters, a former political protester who had been active in the Free Speech Movement. Taking to heart the movement's condemnation of the "plastic" character of the American mass-consumption culture, Waters set out to create a new California cuisine, based on healthy, often organic, locally grown ingredients and prepared and served in an informal setting by culinary craftspeople. The result was Chez Panisse, perhaps the most influential American restaurant of the late twentieth century. Located in the North Shattuck business district, Chez Panisse became the cornerstone of a complex of nearby culinary establishments, including Peet's Coffee, the French Hotel, the collectively owned and operated Cheese Board, and a number of other specialty food and service enterprises. By the time an upscale Andronico's supermarket moved into the former site of the Shattuck Avenue Co-op in the late eighties, North Berkeley's Gourmet Ghetto had long since come of age. Similar developments occurred in shopping areas in other well-heeled neighborhoods, particularly Solano Avenue and the Elmwood-Rockridge district in south Berkeley. Indeed, Elmwood residents finally demanded a zoning ordinance limiting the number of restaurants along College Avenue to preserve the retail character of their neighborhood business district.

Consistent with her egalitarian beliefs, Alice Waters started the Edible Schoolyard garden project at Martin Luther King Middle School and opened an inexpensive take-out restaurant on San Pablo Avenue. But California cuisine was never cheap, and Chez Panisse in particular appealed to an affluent clientele. Patrons were more likely to arrive at the restaurant in stretch limos than VW vans. Meanwhile, a former Peet's employee, who had learned some valuable lessons about the yuppie market while working in Berkeley, moved to Seattle and established Starbucks, a chain of ubiquitous coffee houses that eventually became a part of the same corporate, mass-consumption culture the sixties activists had loved to hate.

The most prosperous new Berkeley retail area in the 1980s and 90s was Fourth Street, a collection of tasteful shops located on two West Berkeley blocks next to the railroad tracks north of Hearst Avenue. Established by the developers Denny Abrams and Rick Millikin, the district, in typical nouveau Berkeley style, was initially anchored by two popular eating establishments, the Fourth Street Grill and Bette's Ocean View Diner. Just off the freeway, Fourth Street became a destination for affluent shoppers from around the Bay Area seeking an alternative to chain stores and suburban malls. Fourth Street was the most obvious example of West Berkeley gentrification, a process that included the transformation of several old industrial buildings into office and loft space.

Less than a block south of the Fourth Street shopping complex, Spenger's Fish Grotto and Restaurant, a Berkeley institution for more than a century, was unable to adjust to the new era.

Begun as a tiny crab stand and bar by Johann Spenger in 1890, the establishment grew into one of the East Bay's most popular eateries. At one time, Spenger's operated its own fishing fleet and served more meals than any other restaurant west of the Mississippi. Several generations of East Bay residents enjoyed family dinners in the restaurant's maze of dark dining rooms. But in 1998 Johann's aged grandson announced that the restaurant was losing money and would close. Food critics commented that the Spenger family had been unable to keep up with the times and was unwilling to adjust the restaurant's menu to the tastes of a new generation influenced by California cuisine.

The 150 jobs lost at Spenger's were offset many times over by the new restaurant boom of the eighties and nineties. But whereas Spenger's jobs had been covered by collective-bargaining contracts, virtually all the fashionable new Berkeley restaurants and shops, like most of the new biotech and software firms, were nonunion. Indeed, when Spenger's reopened in 2000 under new management provided by a national chain, the revived restaurant was also nonunion. Trade unions survived as an important part of Berkeley's economy in the early twenty-first century only because California public employees won collective-bargaining rights in the 1970s. School-district employees staged a major strike in 1975, and city government and community-college workers, as well as clerical and blue-collar employees at the university, also unionized during that decade. The biggest labor dispute of the 1990s was a successful campaign by Cal teaching assistants to win collective-bargaining rights.

ETHNIC DIVERSITY

Among the workers who lost their jobs at Spenger's were Mexican immigrants from the state of Michoacán. For more than three decades, they had been coming to work at the restaurant, often crossing and recrossing the border many times over the years. They moved into other Berkeley service occupations and helped establish a significant Latino presence in the Ocean View neighborhood adjacent to Spenger's, where earlier generations of European immigrants had once lived. More recently, Berkeley's extensive coffeehouse culture has attracted workers from the Mexican state of Jalisco. Latinos are also an important part of Berkeley's industrial labor force, and immigrant Latina women often work as domestics in affluent Berkeley households. Each weekday morning, mostly Spanish-speaking immigrants line up on street corners near Spenger's to bid for day jobs in construction and gardening. During the 1990s Latinos were one of the fastest-growing segments of the city's population, constituting about 10 percent of the total of slightly more than one hundred thousand Berkeley residents by 2000.

Recent Asian immigration, initiated by a major reform in American immigration law passed by Congress in 1965, has also profoundly affected the city. Portions of University Avenue have emerged as a regional shopping center for people from the Indian subcontinent. By the 1990s, Asian Americans, many of them first- or second-generation immigrants, had become the largest single ethnic group in the university's undergraduate population, making up nearly 40 percent of new freshman students. The important Asian and Asian American presence at UC was symbolized by the choice of the engineering professor Chang-Lin Tien, a Taiwanese immigrant, as Berkeley chancellor in 1990. By 2000 Asians were the second largest ethnic group in Berkeley's population, making up about 17 percent of the total.

But while the city's Latino and Asian American populations increased, and the white population, which made up about 55 percent of the total in 2000, remained stable, African American numbers declined in the 1990s. Some affluent blacks moved to new, multiethnic suburban developments in communities like Hercules and Antioch, while poor and working-class African Americans were often forced out of the city by rapidly escalating housing costs. By the 1980s, many black families who had bought homes after World War II were ready to sell and move to housing more convenient for people of their years. They found plenty of potential middle-class white and Asian buyers who were looking for relative bargains in an inflated real-estate market. White and Asian students and young professionals were also able to outbid black families for flatland rental units. The result was a reintegration of some previously all-black neighborhoods, not so much because of open housing policies as because African American families were unable to compete in the superheated Berkeley housing market.

One source of diversity in the city's population was university affirmative-action policies, used to maintain an ethnically balanced student body. Virtually all affirmative-action students were academically qualified in the sense that they met the university's strict systemwide requirements, which limited admission to the top 12.5 percent of state high-school graduates. But after meeting the systemwide requirements, "underrepresented minority" students received preference for admittance to the prestigious Berkeley campus. This provoked protest from some white and Asian parents whose children were diverted to other UC campuses. In 1995, the university Regent Ward Connerly took up the parents' cause. Supported by Governor Pete Wilson and over the objections of Chancellor Tien, Connerly persuaded the Regents to end affirmative action in the UC system. The following year, Wilson and Connerly led the campaign for Proposition 209, a statewide initiative that extended the ban on affirmative-action policies to all state and local government entities in California. The result was a substantial reduction in the numbers of African American, Latino, and American Indian students at Berkeley. The end of affirmative action may also have been a factor in Tien's 1997 resignation.

PRIVATIZING THE UNIVERSITY

During his term as chancellor, Tien, like his predecessor Ira Michael Heyman, had to deal with a growing financial crunch. Particularly during the recession years of the early nineties, revenues from the state failed to keep pace with increases in university expenditures. By the midnineties, state general-fund allocations covered only 35 percent of the Cal budget. The university responded with huge increases in student fees and major campaigns to attract private contributions. Tien was successful in obtaining large grants from wealthy individuals and corporations, and private funds were an important source of support for the construction of new computer-science and biology facilities.

The Haas School of Business benefited not only from the generosity of the Haas family but also from that of dozens of other major donors. Virtually every room in the new business-school complex seemed to be named after an individual or corporate donor. In 1998 the College of Natural Resources entered into a lucrative contract with the Novartis Corporation, a multinational pharmaceutical company. The college received company funds in return for allowing Novartis first access to the results of university research programs. Of course the university had always depended on private contributions to supplement state spending, but the scale and influence of individual and corporate funding in the 1990s raised serious questions about academic independence and the distinction between public and private institutions.

By the nineties, then, the university was even more integrated into the postindustrial corporate world than it had been in the sixties. Mario Savio's fears were being realized with a vengeance. But student protests in the eighties and nineties were muted at best. In the 1980s, campus activists played a significant role in persuading the city and state governments to withdraw investments that benefited the apartheid regime of South Africa. In the 1990s, the end of affirmative action also provoked protests, and some students were involved in community projects that promoted social change. In general, however, Cal student attitudes reflected a lack of political engagement in society as a whole: personal and career motives seemed more important than political causes. Card tables in Sproul Plaza were more likely to be sponsored by social or religious clubs than by political organizations. Even the American military intervention in Iraq did not substantially change this state of affairs.

Events on campus were important to the wider community because the university continued to be the tail that wagged the Berkeley dog. UC dominated Berkeley's economy and was by far the city's largest employer. The university's workforce, of about fifteen thousand employees, was larger than all of those for the city's next eight largest employers combined. The Sedway Group, a San Francisco economic research firm, estimated that in the 1998–99 academic year, Cal students spent $170 million in Berkeley, and UC generated more than $374 million in personal income in the city. In many other, less tangible ways, including the influence of its museums, cultural performances, and athletic events, the university exerted a mighty influence on the city's character and life.

TELEGRAPH AVENUE

It was hardly surprising, then, that both the university administration and the city government were deeply concerned about the state of Telegraph Avenue, the best-known meeting place of town and gown. Telegraph was arguably a thriving business district serving university students and out-of-town visitors. The Avenue was home to some of the city's most important commercial institutions, including Moe's and Cody's bookstores. But it was also the Main Street of a troubled community that reflected some of the most serious social problems of contemporary America.

In the sixties, Telegraph Avenue street people were often young adventurers testing the frontiers of the countercultural experience. By the eighties, street people were more likely to be impoverished and homeless, sometimes plagued by drug and alcohol abuse. In the mideighties, restless young African Americans hung out on the Avenue, and in the nineties, young, homeless whites established themselves in the area. The future of People's Park continued to be a matter of intense debate and the park itself a place of more than occasional conflict. Merchants and neighborhood residents periodically demanded an end to what they called antisocial behavior, and city and university officials usually responded with a combination of police crackdowns and social programs that were supposed to deal with unmet community needs. Predictably, neither the crackdowns nor the programs resolved issues that reflected deep national problems of poverty and homelessness. For Telegraph Avenue business interests, the trick was to demand city action without making conditions sound so bad that potential customers would be scared away. Conversely, if the Avenue were cleaned up too much, it might alienate the customers for whom the area's unconventional atmosphere was a definite attraction. The closing of Cody's Books on Telegraph in 2006 focused attention on the district's problems and brought new promises of city action. (Cody's continued to operate its Fourth Street store.)

DOWNTOWN

In the late 1990s one of the unintended consequences of police crackdowns on Telegraph was that some homeless young people relocated themselves to the plaza adjacent to the Shattuck Avenue BART station. This was hardly what the mayor, Shirley Dean, had in mind, as she was leading an energetic attempt to spruce up downtown Berkeley and improve its image. Like old central business districts all over America, downtown Berkeley had a tough time competing with automobile-oriented shopping malls. In the 1950s and 60s, El Cerrito Plaza took business away from downtown. In the seventies and early eighties, the villain was Richmond's giant Hilltop Plaza, and by the nineties, Emeryville's reincarnation as a regional shopping center took its toll. Yet downtown Berkeley showed remarkable resilience, fighting to remain a viable commercial district without going through an expensive redevelopment process that would have transformed the area beyond recognition. The BART station and proximity to the UC campus helped, as did the downtown locations of city government, Berkeley High, and Vista College. Most important, perhaps, was the resistance of many Berkeleyans to the idea of a commercial culture centered on "plastic" shopping malls.

Local concern did not prevent the demise of many old Berkeley downtown businesses. In the 1980s, for example, the Hink's department store closed after more than sixty years in operation, but it was replaced by a multiscreen movie theater, assuring that Shattuck Avenue would remain an important entertainment center. In the nineties, Edy's restaurant and ice cream parlor also succumbed, giving way to an upscale Eddie Bauer clothing store (which subsequently closed in the midst of the company's financial meltdown). These changes were part of a larger trend of downtown commercial occupation by national chains, including

Ross Stores, Barnes and Noble Books, and Blockbuster Video. In one case, a well-known national brand, Power Bar, started by a former Cal track athlete, Brian Maxwell, located its headquarters in Berkeley, occupying the Great Western Building and placing a giant neon sign on the roof. Some of downtown was decidedly scruffy, and many of the old buildings were in serious need of seismic upgrading. But in the nineties, private developers were willing to invest in several new downtown structures.

The most important of the new developers was Patrick Kennedy, a politically connected Piedmont businessman who built several new Berkeley buildings combining commercial and residential uses. His most controversial structure was the massive Gaia Building on Allston Way, which took full advantage of various zoning exceptions and incentives to rise well above the normal city height limits. Kennedy's projects were strongly supported by "ecocity" enthusiasts like Richard Register, who argued that denser development would preserve open space and promote more walking and public-transit use. Opponents, including some of the framers of the original 1973 Neighborhood Preservation Ordinance, were equally convinced that Berkeley was already too congested and needed stricter building height and bulk limits. By 2004 the building boom, combined with a regional economic downturn, produced something not seen in Berkeley since the 1980s: "for rent" signs on local apartment buildings.

While the debate continued, the public sector fully participated in downtown development. The city subsidized some of the new private construction and embarked on a downtown building boom of its own, including a major expansion of the central library, construction of a new police headquarters, and a substantial retrofit of the Civic Center Building. After supporters of Vista College threatened to establish a separate community-college district for Berkeley, Albany, and Emeryville, the Peralta Community College District finally agreed to build a substantial new downtown building for Vista on Center Street. City politicians and business leaders favored a proposal to rename the institution, and in 2006 "Berkeley City College" moved into its new Center Street location. The Berkeley Repertory Theater, which won a Tony award for regional drama in 1997, dramatically expanded its facilities, making a major contribution to the city's plan to transform Addison Street into an official "cultural district." The Aurora Theater and the Jazzschool located their facilities on Addison, and the Freight and Salvage nightclub planned to move into the neighborhood. This activity, in turn, stimulated the opening of new upscale restaurants in the vicinity.

The university also proposed substantial downtown development, including a hotel and conference center and a museum complex. In 2005 the city dropped a lawsuit challenging the environmental impact report for the university physical expansion outlined in a Long Range Development Plan in return for UC's agreement to partner with the city in a joint downtown planning process. For development critics, including the *Berkeley Daily Planet*, this was the equivalent of letting the fox guard the chicken coop, but the city had little bargaining power. Under state law, UC is exempt from paying local taxes and from city zoning and other land-use policies. Much to the critics' dismay, Mayor Tom Bates argued that the agreement with the UC chancellor, Robert Birgeneau, was the best deal the city could get.

COMMON GROUND

In spite of its problems, downtown Berkeley continued to serve many of its historic purposes: transit hub, government center, central business district and, above all, common ground for a diverse community. It was the one major commercial district that still catered to working-class families; and restaurants, the Berkeley Rep, and the weekly farmers' market also appealed to middle- and upper-middle-class consumers. At lunchtime, UC students on their way to BART and workers from university and city offices shared sidewalks with throngs of Berkeley High kids, shoppers at Walgreens and Ross, and homeless people seeking handouts. It was not always pretty, but it was a diverse cross-section of Berkeley society.

And it definitely was not a suburban mall. Postwar suburbs were often homogeneous in terms of race, class, and lifestyle, but traditional American cities like Berkeley have historically been unruly collections of diverse people and neighborhoods. Joseph Lyford, a UC journalism professor, called Berkeley an "archipelago," a chain of separate social and cultural islands. In some respects this is what the city has been ever since Ocean View was forced to coexist with the campus community in the early 1870s. Cities like Berkeley need common ground, not just in the physical sense of a central business district, but also in the intellectual and cultural sense of common visions, experiences, and institutions that build bridges between the separate islands of neighborhood, race, and class. In the very early twenty-first century, in the midst of an age of inequality, such community ties are all the more important. And many optimistic citizens of Berkeley argue that the ties still exist, that the traumatic economic and social changes of recent years have stretched but still not torn the city's fabric.

Berkeley history has often been a dialogue between the practical realities of the times and the hopes and dreams of the city's most idealistic residents. Back in the sixties, the underground radio newscaster Scoop Nisker used to tell his listeners that if they didn't like the news he was reporting, they should go out and make some news of their own. There are still people in Berkeley willing to take Nisker's advice, willing to challenge the popular assumptions and practical realities of the day and make some new and better Berkeley history of their own.

PLATES

IMAGES FROM THE BERKELEY PUBLIC LIBRARY COLLECTIONS

The Berkeley Public Library had its origins in efforts to tame the city's often rowdy working-class youth. Reformers argued that libraries were better places for young people to frequent than saloons. In 1892 two recent Cal graduates, John Kelsey, a pharmacist, and William Waste, a future California Supreme Court justice, cooperated with John Layman, a UC librarian, and the Women's Christian Temperance Union to open a public reading room in space donated by Francis Kittredge Shattuck. In 1895 the city government agreed to support the project with public funds. Ten years later a grant from the Carnegie Foundation allowed the city to construct a library building on land donated by Rosa Shattuck, Francis's wife. That structure was replaced by the old wing of the present main library branch in 1931, and the city retrofitted and greatly expanded the complex in 2002. By then the library system also included four neighborhood branches.

The library may well be the most popular institution of local government. Berkeley has one of the highest per capita rates of library usage in the country, and since the 1980s voters have

backed a special tax for library operations. Library policy deci-
sions, including changes in schedules and the introduction of new
technologies, provoke impassioned public debate. One of the most
encouraging and attractive qualities of Berkeley life is the care and
concern the community has for its library system.

The 2002 retrofitting and new construction project included
building a Berkeley History Room in the main branch. The new
space allowed greater public access to the library's valuable collection of historical documents, including photographs, posters,
and other illustrations. The heart of the picture collection is a large
group of photos gathered and donated by the late John Swingle,
a former bookseller and city council member. Many of the following pictures come from the Swingle Collection. Others are
from a group of photographs documenting the 1969 People's Park
struggle taken by former librarian Sayre Van Young.

Finally, I have included some of the pictures gathered from the
public by the South Berkeley library branch in the 1990s. The library invited South Berkeley residents to donate photographs
from dresser drawers and family albums for a public exhibit on
the area's life and history. The result is a remarkable collection
of professional studio shots, official school and organization photos, and informal family snapshots. The pictures document life in
Berkeley's most ethnically and culturally diverse neighborhood
during the first half of the twentieth century. The South Berkeley photographs and the other illustrations in this section of the
book are reminders that local history is not only the story of
prominent movers and shakers. It also includes the impact of
everyday lives, the actions and reactions of residents like those who
emerge from the anonymity of the past by virtue of images preserved by the Berkeley Public Library.

PLATE 1. New Berkeley Public Library, Shattuck Ave., ca. 1931. Note the street Christmas decorations.

PLATE 2. The San Francisco Bay, Oakland, and Berkeley, from Claremont Heights, 1890.

PLATE 3. J. K. Stewart's store, Shattuck Ave. and Dwight Way, ca. 1880.

PLATE 4. Acheson Hotel, Shattuck Ave. and University Ave., 1892.

PLATE 5. and 6. Berkeley branch line steam train on Shattuck Ave. looking north toward University Ave., with Berkeley station in the right foreground, 1888 and 1898. Note the extensive development of downtown during the intervening decade.

PLATE 7. and 8. Allston Way, looking east from Shattuck Ave., 1888 and 1898, again showing extensive development during the ten-year period.

PLATE 9. Downtown businesses on the west side of Shattuck Ave. between Addison St. and University Ave., ca. 1890.

PLATE 10. Looking east on Vine St. from Shattuck Ave., 1898. The area developed when the Berkeley branch line was extended to Berryman Station. The building on the right still stands and was restored to its original appearance in the 1990s.

PLATE 11. Deaf and Blind School, now the site of the Clark Kerr Campus, 1898.

PLATE 12. Berthelson's Motor Cycle Garage, West Berkeley, 1915. Note policeman in the crowd. Under Chief August Vollmer, Berkeley's force was one of the first to motorize.

PLATE 13. Arrival of the Auto Age. Car traffic, Center St. and Shattuck Ave., ca. 1920. The building on the left was demolished to make way for the current downtown branch of the Bank of America.

PLATE 14. and 15. Devastation in the North Gate neighborhood north of campus in the aftermath of the 1923 firestorm. More than 500 buildings were destroyed in a preview of the even larger 1991 Oakland/Berkeley Hills fire.

PLATE 16. View from the hills with the university campus in the foreground, 1889. Note the eucalyptus trees, most planted about twenty years earlier. The grove on the west side of the campus still stands and contains some of the largest eucalyptus trees in North America.

PLATE 17. Campus viewed from the west, 1901. Of the buildings shown, only South Hall on the right still stands. It and North Hall, on the left, were the first two structures on campus when the university moved to Berkeley in 1873. North Hall is now the site of the Doe Library annex.

PLATE 18. Bacon Hall, housing the university art gallery and library, 1898.

PLATE 19. University library interior, Bacon Hall, 1898.

PLATE 20. Young women, probably students, on campus, 1905. By 1911 women made up 40 percent of UC students.

PLATE 21. University cadet band, 1914. The cadets were the precursors of today's ROTC.

PLATE 22. Cal football practice, ca. 1930.

PLATE 23. South Berkeley resident, all dressed up for the holiday, July 4, 1916.

PLATE 24. South Berkeley family snapshot, 1924. At the beginning of the twentieth century, the development of the Kodak Brownie camera began the era of snapshots, pictures taken by everyday people rather than professional photographers.

PLATE 25. South Berkeley kids put on a show, ca. 1920s.

PLATE 26. and 27. Japanese American families, South Berkeley, ca. 1920s. Before World War II, virtually all of the city's Asian and Asian American population was concentrated in South Berkeley.

PLATE 28. and 29. African American families, South Berkeley, ca. 1940s. Restrictive covenants and other discriminatory practices kept African Americans and Asians in the southwestern sections of the city.

PLATE 30. Lincoln School's multiethnic graduating class, 1938.

PLATE 31. South Berkeley traffic boys. The traffic patrol grew out of chief August Vollmer's "junior police," started in the early twentieth century as a way to fight juvenile delinquency.

PLATE 32. Nissei Babes championship basketball team, 1938. South Berkeley Japanese American community organizations had extensive social and athletic youth programs.

PLATE 33. South Berkeley sisters, ca. late 1930s. More than 1,500 Berkeleyans were interned by the federal government's relocation program during World War II.

PLATE 34. Berkeley factory workers on a break, ca. late 1930s.

PLATE 35. Berkeley
soldier, probably during
World War II.

PLATE 36. South Berkeley wedding, 1946.

PLATE 37. Family members on South Berkeley street, ca. early 1950s.

PLATE 38. Lady with Thunderbird, South Berkeley, 1963.

PLATE 39. View from the hills, 1948. As this photo illustrates, by the 1940s Berkeley was already built-out and filled-in. The biggest physical changes since then have been the massive expansion of the university and the equally massive growth of bay fill, largely garbage, to create the current marina and Cesar Chavez Park.

PLATE 40. National Guard occupying Berkeley, People's Park conflict, 1969. People's Park generated the largest of all the famous Berkeley protests of the sixties.

PLATE 41. People's Park under military control, 1969.

PLATE 42. Demonstrators on Shattuck Ave., People's Park conflict, 1969.

PLATE 43. Protest flier on bayonet, People's Park controversy, 1969.

PLATE 44. Giving peace a chance. Young guardsmen and Berkeley residents posing together, People's Park controversy, 1969. The Berkeleyan at right is wearing his guardsman companion's helmet.

BIBLIOGRAPHY

Albrier, Frances Mary. "Advocate for Racial Equality." Transcripts of interviews by Malca Chall, 1977, 1978. Regional Oral History Office, The Bancroft Library, University of California, Berkeley.

Aronovici, John. *Quick Index to the Origin of Berkeley's Names.* Berkeley: Berkeley Historical Society, 2004.

Bach, Eve. *The Cities' Wealth: Programs for Community Economic Control in Berkeley, California.* Washington, DC: National Conference on Alternative State and Local Public Policies, 1976.

Berkeley Art Center. *A History of Berkeley.* Berkeley: Berkeley Art Center, 1978.

———. *The Whole World's Watching: Peace and Social Justice Movements of the 1960s and 1970s.* Berkeley: Berkeley Art Center, 2001.

Berkeley Historical Society. "History of the Consumers Cooperative of Berkeley." Interviews by Therese Pipe, 1977–1983. Berkeley.

Berkeley History Book Committee. *Looking Back at Berkeley: A Pictorial History of a Diverse City.* Berkeley: Berkeley Historical Society, 1984.

Bernhardi, Robert. *The Buildings of Berkeley.* Berkeley: Lederer, Street, and Zeus, 1971.

Boutelle, Sarah Holmes. *Julia Morgan, Architect.* New York: Abbeville Press, 1995.

Bowman, Jacobin. "The Peraltas and Their Houses." *California Historical Society Quarterly* 30, no. 3 (December 1952): 217–31.

Brown, Elaine. *A Taste of Power: A Black Woman's Story.* New York: Pantheon, 1992.

Brucker, Gene, Henry F. May, and David A. Hollinger. *History at Berkeley: A Dialog in Three Parts.* Berkeley: Institute of Governmental Studies, 1998.

Cardwell, Kenneth. *Bernard Maybeck: Artisan, Architect, Artist.* Santa Barbara, CA: Peregrine Smith, 1977.

Cerny, Susan Dinkelspiel. *Berkeley Landmarks: An Illustrated Guide to Berkeley, California's Architectural Heritage.* Berkeley: Berkeley Architectural Heritage Association, 1994.

———. *Northside: Historic Survey of a North Berkeley Neighborhood before and after the 1923 Wildfire.* Berkeley: Berkeley Architectural Heritage Association, 1990.

Chavez, Lydia. *The Color Bind: California's Battle to End Affirmative Action.* Berkeley: University of California Press, 1998.

Chronicle of the University of California, various issues.

Clifford, Geraldine Jonçich. *Equally in View: The University of California, Its Women, and the Schools.* Berkeley: Institute of Governmental Studies, 1995.

Crane, Clarkson. *The Western Shore.* Salt Lake City, UT: G. M. Smith, 1985.

Crouchett, Lawrence, Lonnie G. Brunch III, and Martha Kendall Winnacker. *Visions toward Tomorrow: The History of the East Bay Afro-American Community, 1852–1977.* Oakland: Northern California Center for Afro-American History and Life, 1989.

———. *William Byron Rumford: The Life and Public Services of a California Legislator.* El Cerrito, CA: Downey Place, 1984.

Davidson, Sara. *Loose Change: Three Women of the Sixties.* Garden City, NY: Doubleday, 1977.

Davis, Nuel Phar. *Lawrence and Oppenheimer.* New York: Simon and Schuster, 1968.

Douglass, John Aubrey. *The California Idea and American Higher Education.* Stanford, CA: Stanford University Press, 2000.

Federal Writers Program, Works Projects Administration. *Berkeley: The First Seventy-five Years.* Berkeley: Gillick Press, 1941.

Ferrier, William Warren. *Berkeley, California: The Story of the Evolution of a*

Hamlet into a City of Culture and Commerce. Berkeley: Sather Gate Bookstore, 1933.

―――. *Origins and Development of the University of California.* Berkeley: Sather Gate Bookstore, 1930.

Gardner, David. *The California Loyalty Oath Controversy.* Berkeley: University of California Press, 1967.

Gates, Barbara. *Already Home: A Topography of Spirit and Place.* Boston: Shambhala, 2003.

Goines, David Lance. *The Free Speech Movement: Coming of Age in the 1960s.* Berkeley: Ten Speed Press, 1993.

Harvey, James. *The University and the City.* Berkeley: University of California, Bureau of Public Administration, 1958.

Heilbron, John L., and Robert Seidel. *Lawrence and His Laboratory: A History of the Lawrence Berkeley Laboratory.* Berkeley: University of California Press, 1989.

Helfand, Harvey. *University of California, Berkeley: The Campus Guide.* New York: Princeton Architectural Press, 2002.

Holliday, J. S., *The World Rushed In: The California Gold Rush Experience.* New York: Simon and Schuster, 1981.

Hutchinson, Fred. *Street Names of the City of Berkeley.* Berkeley: Berkeley Public Library, 1962.

Jones, William Carey. *Illustrated History of the University of California.* Berkeley: Students Cooperative Society, 1901.

Jorgensen-Ismaili, Karen. *A Teacher's Guide to Primary Resources on Berkeley History.* Berkeley: Berkeley Historical Society, 1983.

Kerr, Clark. *The Gold and the Blue: A Personal Memoir of the University of California.* 2 vols. Berkeley: University of California Press, 2001–2.

Kirk, Anthony. *Founded by the Bay: The History of the Macaulay Foundry, 1896–1996.* Berkeley: Macaulay Foundry, 1996.

La France, Danielle. *Berkeley: A Literary Tribute.* Berkeley: Heyday, 1997.

Lasar, Matthew. *Pacifica Radio: The Rise of an Alternative Network.* Philadelphia: Temple University Press, 1999.

Lemke-Santangelo, Gretchen. *Abiding Courage: African American Migrant Women in the East Bay.* Chapel Hill: University of North Carolina Press, 1996.

Lipset, Seymour, and Sheldon Wolin, eds. *The Berkeley Student Revolt: Facts and Interpretations*. Garden City, NY: Anchor, 1965.

Longstreth, Richard. *Julia Morgan, Architect*. Berkeley: Berkeley Architectural Heritage Association, 1977.

Lyford, Joseph. *The Berkeley Archipelago*. Chicago: Regnery Gateway, 1982.

Maran, Meredith. *Class Dismissed: A Year in the Life of an American High School*. New York: St. Martin's Press, 2000.

Margolin, Malcolm. *East Bay Out: A Personal Guide to the East Bay Regional Parks*. Berkeley: Heyday, 1988.

———. *The Ohlone Way*. Berkeley: Heyday, 1978.

May, Henry. *Coming to Terms: A Study in Memory and History*. Berkeley: University of California Press, 1988.

———. *Three Faces of Berkeley: Competing Ideologies in the Wheeler Era, 1899–1919*. Berkeley: Institute of Governmental Studies, 1993.

Maybeck, Jacomena. *Maybeck: The Family View*. Berkeley: Berkeley Architectural Heritage Association, 1980.

McCardle, Phil, ed. *Exactly Opposite the Golden Gate: Essays on Berkeley's History*. Berkeley: Berkeley Historical Society, 1986.

Nathan, Harriet, and Stanley Scott, eds. *Experiment and Change in Berkeley*. Berkeley: Institute of Governmental Studies, 1978.

Newton, Huey P., and Bobby Seale. *Seize the Time: The Story of the Black Panther Party*. New York: Random House, 1970.

Noble, John W. *Its Name is MUD*. Oakland: East Bay Municipal Utilities District, 1970.

Partridge, Loren. *John Galen Howard and the Berkeley Campus: Beaux-Arts Architecture in the Athens of the West*. Berkeley: Berkeley Architectural Heritage Association, 1978.

Pettitt, George. *Berkeley: The Town and Gown of It*. Berkeley: Howell-North, 1973.

———. *A History of Berkeley*. Oakland: Alameda County Historical Society, 1976.

Pettitt, Kenneth. *Berkeley AnteBellum*. Berkeley: Kenneth Pettitt, 1995.

Pitcher, Donald. *Berkeley Inside Out: A Guide to Restaurants, Entertainment, People, and Politics*. Berkeley: Heyday, 1989.

Schwartz, Richard. *Berkeley 1900: What Daily Life Was Like at the Turn of the Century, As Told by Local Newspaper Articles*. Berkeley: Richard Schwartz, 2000.

————. *Earthquake Exodus, 1906: Berkeley Responds to the San Francisco Refugees.* Berkeley: RSB, 2006.

Scott, Mel. *The San Francisco Bay Area: A Metropolis in Perspective.* Berkeley: University of California Press, 1959.

Sedway Group. *Building the Bay Area's Future: A Study of the Economic Impact of the University of California, Berkeley.* Berkeley: University of California, 2001.

Sibley, Carol. *Never a Dull Moment.* Berkeley: Documentation and Evaluation of Special Projects in Schools, 1972.

Stadtman, Verne. *The University of California, 1868–1968.* New York: McGraw-Hill, 1970.

Stein, Mimi. *A Vision Achieved: Fifty Years of the East Bay Regional Park District.* Oakland: East Bay Regional Park District, 1984.

Stone, Irving, ed. *There Was Light: Autobiography of a University.* Garden City, NY: Doubleday, 1970.

Sullivan, Neil. *Now Is the Time: Integration in the Berkeley Schools.* Bloomington: University of Indiana Press, 1970.

Uchida, Yoshida. *Desert Exile: The Uprooting of a Japanese American Family.* Seattle: University of Washington Press, 1982.

Van Young, Sayre. *Berkeley: A Selected Annotated Bibliography.* Berkeley: Berkeley Public Library, 1975.

Willes, Burl, ed. *Picturing Berkeley: A Postcard History.* Berkeley: Berkeley Historical Society and Berkeley Architectural Heritage Association, 2002.

Wollenberg, Charles. *Golden Gate Metropolis: Perspectives on Bay Area History.* Berkeley: Institute of Governmental Studies, 1985.

————. *Photographing the Second Gold Rush: Dorothea Lange and the Bay Area at War, 1941–1945.* Berkeley: Heyday, 1995.

Wood, M. W. *History of Alameda County.* Oakland: Pacific Press, 1883.

Woodbridge, Sally. *Bernard Maybeck: Visionary Architect.* New York: Abbeville, 1992.

INDEX

Page numbers in italics refer to illustrations.

DESIGNER
J. G. Braun
TEXT
10/15 Janson
DISPLAY
Interstate
COMPOSITOR
Integrated Composition Systems
INDEXER
Sayre Van Young
PRINTER AND BINDER
Friesens Corporation